RevisionGuide

GCSE ENGLISH
AQA Specification A

Collins · *do brilliantly !*

RevisionGuide

GCSE ENGLISH
AQA Specification A

■ **Keith Brindle**

■ **Series Editor: Jayne de Courcy**

William Collins' dream of knowledge for all began with the publication of his first book in 1819. A self-educated mill worker, he not only enriched millions of lives, but also founded a flourishing publishing house. Today, staying true to this spirit, Collins books are packed with inspiration, innovation and practical expertise. They place you at the centre of a world of possibility and give you exactly what you need to explore it.

Collins. Do more.

Published by Collins

An imprint of HarperCollins*Publishers*

77-85 Fulham Palace Road
London W6 8JB

Browse the complete Collins catalogue at
www.collinseducation.com

© HarperCollins*Publishers* Limited 2005

First published 2005

10 9 8 7 6 5 4 3

ISBN-13 978-0-00-719060-7
ISBN-10 0-00-719060-3

Keith Brindle asserts the moral right to be identified as the author of this work.

British Library Cataloguing in Publication Data
A catalogue record for this publication is available from the British Library.

Acknowledgements
The Author and Publishers are grateful to the following for permission to reproduce copyright material:
'Mother of truant sent back to prison' by Lucy Ward, Educational Correspondent, The Guardian, 24th March, 2004. Copyright © The Guardian, 2004. Used with permission. 'Youngsters want their mums to be like Marge' by Ruth Gledhill, The Times, March 17th, 2004. © NI Syndication, London 2004. Reprinted with permission. Extract from 'Sky The Magazine' October 2003. Reprinted with permission. 'Muller puds advertorial' reprinted with the kind permission of Muller Group UK. Extract from 'Gaze and Laze', from Take A Break Magazine, 20th November, 2003. Reprinted with permission of Bauer UK. Extract from ''Toxic' Rust-Bucket is Here' The Sun, 13th November, 2003. Reprinted with permission. 'Nivea for Men' advert. Reprinted with the kind permission of Beiersdorf UK. 'Christina's true story – It's too late for Daniel – but I've saved other teenagers' lives' Best Magazine, 13th April 2004, pg 36, issue 15/04. Courtesy of Best Magazine © National Magazine Company, also reprinted with permission of Christina Anderson, Daniel's mother. Screengrab of www.bbc.co.uk/holiday © BBC. Reprinted with permission of BBC. Charles Causley obituary, first published in The Times Educational Supplement. Reprinted with the kind permission of the author Heather Neill. Article about a couple celebrating their 40th birthdays asking for donations to charity instead of presents, from Yorkshire Evening Post, 15th May, 2003. Reprinted with permission. Vienna advert. © Vienna Tourist Board. Reprinted with permission. 'There is no Spoon' by Phil Hogan, The Observer, 9th November, 2003. © The Observer. Reprinted with permission. Extract from 'A Farewell to Arms' by Ernest Hemingway, published by Jonathan Cape. Used by permission of The Random House Group Limited. Extract from 'Grand Inquisitor' by Robin Day, published by Weidenfeld & Nicholson. Reprinted with permission of The Orion Publishing Group Limited. Extract from 'Nothing's Changed' by Tatamkhulu Afrika. 'Vultures' by Chinua Achebe, from 'Beware Soul Brother' published by Heinemann Educational. 'Search for my Tongue' by Sujata Bhatt, from 'Brunizem' published by Carcanet Press Limited, and reprinted with permission of the publishers. 'Island Man' by Grace Nichols, from 'The Fat Black Woman's Poems' published by Virago in 1984. Copyright © Grace Nichols, 1984, reprinted by permission of Curtis Brown Limited, London, on behalf of Grace Nichols. 'Night of the Scorpion' by Nissim Ezekiel, from Poverty Poems published by OUP India. Reprinted by permission of OUP India, New Delhi. From 'Limbo' by Kamau Braithwaite, from The Arrivants: A New World Trilogy published by OUP in 1973. Reprinted by permission of Oxford University Press. 'Half-Caste' by John Agard, from Get Back Pimple published by Penguin Books 1996. Reprinted by permission of John Agard, c/o Caroline Sheldon Literary Agency. Extract from 'Britain gives £6m to help fight Aids' by Jayne Atherton, Metro News, 2nd December, 2003. Reprinted with permission of Solo Syndication, London. Photo – © Reuters. Extract from 'Families to spend less on gifts at Christmas' and photo, from The Daily Mail, 13th November, 2003. Reprinted with permission of Solo Syndication, London. 'Love After Love' by Derek Walcott, from 'Collected Poems' published by Faber and Faber. Reprinted with permission of Faber and Faber Limited. 'Not My Business' by Niyi Osundare, from Songs of the Seasons published by Heinemann Educational Books, Nigeria, 1990. Reprinted with the kind permission of the author. from 'Unrelated Incidents' by Tom Leonard, from Intimate Voices currently published by Etruscan Books, Devon. Copyright © Tom Leonard. Reprinted with the kind permission of the author. 'Two Scavengers in A Truck, Two Beautiful People In A Mercedes' by Lawrence Ferlinghetti, from These Are My Rivers. Copyright © 1979 by Lawrence Ferlinghetti. Reprinted by permission of New Directions Publishing Corporation. 'What Were They Like?' by Denise Levertov from Selected Poems published by Bloodaxe Books 1986. Reprinted by permission of Pollinger Limited, on behalf of the author and the proprietors, New Directions Publishing Corporation. 'This Room' by Imtiaz Dharker, from I Speak for the Devil published by Bloodaxe Books 2001, and 'Blessing' by Imtiaz Dharker, from Postcards from God published by Bloodaxe Books 1997. Reprinted by permission of the publisher, Bloodaxe Books

Photographs
The Author and Publishers are grateful to the following for permission to reproduce photographs:
Corbis: p. 9; Empics: p. 6; Panos/Sean Sprague: p. 40; Press Association: pp. 123; Rex Features: p. 53

Illustrations
Sarah Wimperis

Every effort has been made to contact the holders of copyright material, but if any have been inadvertently overlooked, the Publishers will be pleased to make the necessary arrangements at the first opportunity.

Edited by Sandy Strong
Series and book design by Sally Boothroyd
Photo research by Thelma Gilbert
Permissions by Jackie Newman
Index compiled by Julie Rimington
Production by Katie Butler
Printed and bound by Martins the Printers, Berwick upon Tweed

You might also like to visit
www.harpercollins.co.uk
The book lover's website

CONTENTS AND REVISION PLANNER

ABOUT THIS BOOK

We have planned this book to make your revision as active and effective as possible.

How?

- by breaking down the skills revision into manageable chunks (Revision Sessions)

- by testing your understanding at every step of the way (Check Yourself Questions)

- by providing extra information to help you aim for the very top grade (A* Extras)

- by providing lots of examples of student answers at different levels with comments on them (Good Points)

- by giving you expert examiner's guidance about exam technique (Exam Practice)

Revision Sessions

- There are two main skills that you need to revise for your written AQA Specification A exam: **Reading and Writing**.

- Both of these skills are divided into a number of **short revision sessions**. You should be able to read through each of these in no more than 30 minutes. That is the maximum amount of time that you should spend on revising without taking a short break.

- We have included *What you will be assessed on* pages at the start of Units 1–4. These introductions explain clearly what examiners are looking for when awarding marks, and provide a link to each revision session.

CHECK YOURSELF QUESTIONS

- At the end of each revision session there are one or two Check Yourself Questions. By trying these questions, you will immediately find out whether you have understood and remembered what you have read in the revision session. **Answers** are at the back of the book, along with **extra hints and guidance** on how to achieve high marks.

- If you answer the Check Yourself Questions for a session well, then you can confidently tick off this skill in the 'Revised & understood' box provided in the Contents list. If not, you will need to tick the 'Revise again' box to remind yourself to return to this skill later in your revision programme.

⚡ A* EXTRA

These boxes occur in most of the revision sessions. They highlight what you need to do in order to demonstrate that particular skill at **a very high level**. This will help you to achieve the highest grades in your exam.

Students' Answers and Examiner's Comments

Every revision session includes extracts from students' answers. The **Good Points** box provides examiner's comments on the answers, showing where marks would be scored. In **Types of Writing** Unit 4 (pages 84–119), these answers are provided at C grade and A/A* grade so that you can see what you need to do to raise an answer to the highest level.

Exam Practice

- Unit 5 contains a complete Paper 1 and Paper 2 in the style of the AQA Specification A exam. It will give you **invaluable practice** in answering exam questions well.

- The author, who is an examiner, has provided **clear mark schemes**, based on those used by examiners, which you can mark your own answers against.

- There are also some **sample students' answers with examiner's comments** on them, showing where the students gained and lost marks. Reading through these will help you get a very clear idea of what you need to do in order to score maximum marks when answering questions in your exam.

- Working through this unit will give you an excellent grounding in exam technique.

ABOUT YOUR AQA/A ENGLISH EXAM

Assessment objectives

The examiners set examination questions based on assessment objectives. This book covers all the assessment objectives for Reading and Writing. (Speaking and Listening skills are tested in your coursework, along with some Reading and Writing skills.)

Assessment objectives for Reading

You have to demonstrate your ability to:

* read, with insight and engagement, making appropriate references to texts and developing and sustaining interpretations of them
* distinguish between fact and opinion and evaluate how information is presented
* follow an argument, identifying implications and recognising inconsistencies
* select material appropriate to purpose, collate material from different sources, and make cross references
* understand and evaluate how writers use linguistic, structural and presentational devices to achieve their effects, and comment on ways language varies and changes.

These skills are covered in Units 1 and 2 of this book: *Reading Media and Non-Fiction* and *Poetry from Different Cultures and Traditions.*

Assessment objectives for Writing

You have to demonstrate your ability to:

* communicate clearly and imaginatively, using and adapting form for different readers and purposes
* organise ideas into sentences, paragraphs and whole texts using a variety of linguistic and structural features
* use a range of sentence structures effectively, and with accurate punctuation and spelling.

These skills are covered in Units 3 and 4: *Writing Skills* and *Types of Writing.*

Your exam papers

These assessment objectives are tested in two exam papers:

Paper 1: 1 hour 45 minutes

* Section A: Reading - 1 hour
  You will have to read two or three media and/or non-fiction texts which you have not seen before, and answer a number of questions on them.

* Section B: Writing - 45 minutes
  You will have to choose one title from the four that are offered. You will have to write to argue, persuade or advise the reader.

Paper 2: 1 hour 30 minutes

* Section A: Reading - 45 minutes
  You will have to answer a question on *Poetry from Different Cultures and Traditions*, choosing one from the two that are offered. The question will ask you to compare two poems from those you have studied in the Anthology.

* Section B: Writing - 45 minutes
  Again, you will be offered four titles and will have to respond to just one of them. This time, you will be writing to inform, explain or describe.

Complete practice papers are contained in the Exam Practice section of this book.

GCSE ENGLISH
AQA Specification A

READING MEDIA AND NON-FICTION

What you will be assessed on

Paper 1, Section A will focus on previously unseen texts from the media and possibly other forms of non-fiction. You will have to deal with two or three different texts.

In an hour, you will have to answer about 4–6 questions.

This section of the exam counts for 15% of your total mark.

The unseen texts

- At least one text will be a media text. You might be given, for instance: an article or editorial, a report, advertisement, web page, obituary, advice sheet or leaflet.

- There could also be a non-fiction text which is not from the media such as an extract from a biography or autobiography, a section from an instructional book or an information text.

The questions you will be asked

- Questions will be phrased differently each year, but they will be based on assessment objectives. Some questions will test more than one objective, but within the Section you will be tested on your ability to:

1. *Read, with insight and engagement, making appropriate references to texts and developing and sustaining interpretations of them*

   You will be expected to understand the literal meaning of texts, so that you can explain their content and recognise their form. However, you will also be expected to understand their purpose and recognise their target audience, and to write about how far their aims are achieved. Your views need to be supported by evidence from the texts; and your explanations should be detailed and range across the texts.

   - See Sessions 1-7

2. *Distinguish between fact and opinion and evaluate how information is presented*

   The exam paper will expect you to locate facts and opinions and be able to explain how they have been used by the writer and why. You will be dealing with their purpose in the text and their effect on the reader. To 'evaluate' how information is presented you must give an opinion on how successfully such features have been used.

   - See Session 1

3. *Follow an argument, identifying implications and recognising inconsistencies*

    As well as understanding what a writer says, and in what order, you are likely to have to explain how the argument has been put together: how the writer has used contrasts, anecdotes, humour, exaggeration, evidence and so on. To 'identify implications', you might well have to write about what the writer is suggesting rather than clearly stating; and 'recognising inconsistencies' means dealing with any apparent contradictions in arguments.

    - See Session 2

4. *Understand and evaluate how writers use linguistic, structural and presentational devices to achieve their effects, and comment on ways language varies and changes*

    You will be asked about language, and how it is used to create an effect and further the writer's purpose. You will be writing about whether the language used is appropriate for a particular purpose or audience. Similarly, there will be a question on presentational devices; and you might also be asked about the structure of a text, in terms of either general layout, or how it has been organised.

    - See Sessions 3 and 4

5. *Select material appropriate to your purpose, collate material from different sources and make cross references*

    You will have to refer appropriately to the texts to provide evidence of what you say and you will have to compare elements of at least two texts. This will mean identifying and clearly comparing how writers use particular devices, which means you could be asked to compare arguments or the use of language, facts and opinions, presentational devices or layout.

    - See Sessions 5, 6 and 7

Fact and opinion

In Section A of Paper 1, you will be asked to **distinguish between fact and opinion** in one or more texts and to evaluate how information is presented.

In practice, this is likely to mean you will be expected to:

- locate facts and opinions
- write about how they are used in relation to purpose and audience

and, possibly, to:

- compare the use of fact and opinion in two different texts.

◉ Locating facts and opinions

- **Fact** is what we know to be true. Usually, there is evidence to back it up, so that it can be proved.

- **Opinion** is someone's belief. It is likely to be someone's interpretation of events or details.

- Many texts are a mixture of fact and opinion, as in the article below from *Sky The Magazine*. The facts (and their annotations) are in blue. The opinions (and their annotations) are in orange.

The show that chronicles celeb misbehaviour is back with a swagger **this month,** catching more stars up to some despicable and downright dastardly antics.

The first episode of 'Behaving Badly 3' is a real stunner, with A-listers **Madonna, Christina Aguilera, P Diddy and even** squeaky-clean **David Beckham** having their madder moments exposed to the nation. **Look out for** Hollywood bad boy **Colin Farrell and Britney Spears** up to no good too…

It is true that the show is returning.

The 'antics' might not seem so bad to some.

The stars are famous and things about them will be revealed.

Whether the show is a 'stunner', Beckham is 'squeaky clean', Farrell is bad or Britney up to no good is someone's opinion.

A student writing about the use of facts and opinions in this extract wrote …

The writer's purpose is to persuade viewers to watch the programme, so the facts about who will be appearing are surrounded by opinions on the nature of the programme (it's 'back with a swagger'), the stars ('squeaky clean') and the nature of the material ('downright dastardly antics')…

GOOD POINTS:

- The use of fact and opinion is linked to the purpose of the text. This helps you focus on *why* fact and opinion have been used in a particular way.
- Examples are used to support the ideas.

⚡ A* EXTRA

▸ Top candidates link the use of fact and opinion with the writer's overall purpose, e.g. *Since the writer begins with a series of facts, which persuades us that… and returns to a similar approach at the end…, we are led to believe that…*

▸ In order to link your ideas in this way, you need to plan your answer carefully before you start writing.

- In this extract from the *Yorkshire Evening Post*, the writer has used facts and opinions to achieve a different purpose.

- The writer does not try to dramatise the situation. The facts outweigh the opinions, and are used to make the opinions believable.

Look at the annotations carefully:

> ## A couple celebrating their 40th birthdays have asked for donations to charity instead of presents.
>
> Graham and Chris Lingard of Ilkley both support Christian Aid, the churches' charity which raises money to help struggling Third World countries.
>
> Their birthdays are close to each other and they decided on a joint party as part of this week's nationwide Christian Aid collection week.
>
> Graham said: 'We both wanted to highlight how unfair our world is, and support a charity that works to help change this injustice.
>
> 'The problems facing Africa are hard for us even to imagine. Currently – due to chronic poverty, coupled with recurring drought – 38 million people simply do not have enough to eat. HIV-related illnesses killed 2.4 million people in Africa in 2002,' he said.

The article opens with straightforward facts. This is because it comes from a newspaper and is reporting, rather than trying to 'sell' something to the reader.

The writer includes opinions from Graham.

Graham has given some facts to encourage people to support them.

◎ Comparing texts

- If you are asked to compare the use of fact and opinion in two texts, the easiest way is to:
  - write about the first text
  - write about the second text
  - make comparisons between the two as you deal with the second one.

For example, a student comparing the use of facts and opinions in these two articles began her paragraphs like this ...

> The first text relies heavily on opinions...
>
> Whereas the first text relies so heavily on opinions, the second begins with facts...
>
> The first text makes exaggerated claims, but the second text...
>
> In conclusion...

⚡ A* EXTRA

▶ Top candidates are likely to make value judgements in their comments:
  The report is more effective, not just because of the opinions expressed, but also because of the people who are being quoted...

▶ Their comments will be well balanced and carefully presented.

CHECK YOURSELF QUESTION

Q Use the paragraph openers above to answer this question:
Compare how fact and opinion are used in the articles from *Sky The Magazine* and the *Yorkshire Evening Post*.

Answer is on page 146.

Following an argument

At least one of the questions in Section A of Paper 1 will expect you to demonstrate your ability to follow an argument.

This requires more than simply paraphrasing (putting into your own words) what the writer has said. You will probably be asked to consider the writer's point of view and how the argument has been constructed. This means you need to analyse and comment upon the:
• structure
• language
• techniques.

◎ The writer's point of view

■ Initially, you need to decide what is the writer's attitude to the subject of the text, i.e. his or her point of view. That will help you to clarify the text's purpose. You are making a decision about why it was written.

■ For example, rather than just noting that a text is about the problems facing elderly people, you might need to explain that the writer is supporting the need for more medical help for the aged, or for more funding for senior citizens if they live in the country.

◎ Structure

■ There are many ways to present an argument, but in most cases arguments have:
  • an introduction which sets out the subject of the argument and indicates the writer's viewpoint
  • developed points, designed to prove the writer's case – often, the paragraphs' topic sentences, which come first, will summarise the main points
  • a conclusion, summing up the main reasons why the writer's view is correct – or why the opposing viewpoint is wrong.

■ The writer will take account of the opposite viewpoint, because without that there can be no argument.

■ Look at the way the writer has structured the article below about sport on TV. (The middle four paragraphs have been reduced to just their topic sentences.) Read the annotations carefully, which will help you see the structure:

Paragraph 1 sets out the writer's main point – that he/she feels we are obsessed with sport, and waste much of our lives as a consequence.

Paragraph 2 puts the alternative viewpoint.

What is it that makes people believe that watching sport is the most important activity known to man? Let's face it, we only live for seventy years – eighty if we're lucky – and yet so many people waste so much time watching pretty brainless bodies chasing a ball round a patch of grass; and often spend hundreds of pounds for the privilege. Failing that, they are glued to the game on TV. And when they are dead, what then? A life has been wasted, potential squandered, and nothing has been achieved.

Fans, of course, see it differently…

This line of argument, however, is nothing short of ludicrous…

How many goals do we remember? How many service aces justify the time we spend watching..?

There must, surely, be more we could be doing…

Paragraph 3 mocks the alternative viewpoint.

Paragraphs 4 and 5 develop the argument presented at the start.

So, what is the solution? In Britain we need to change the consciousness of the nation. Firstly, people need educating to realise that we could do more useful things to develop ourselves and – just imagine! – help others. Secondly, we need to remove the cult of the sport star and, instead, lay much more emphasis on those who do something worthwhile. How much better it would be, for example, if children grew up wanting to be a doctor, rather than David Beckham.

Paragraph 6 presents the conclusion – a vision of an improved society, based on the ideas previously stated in the argument. It moves to a final statement of the writer's opinion.

How should you summarise the way the argument has been put together? This is part of what one student wrote ...

The article begins by pointing out that we waste our time watching sport. There is an element of sarcasm (we watch 'pretty brainless bodies chasing a ball') and seem to have no escape at all (we are 'glued', metaphorically, to the game on TV). The message is initially bleak:

'nothing has been achieved'.

However, we move to a conclusion that suggests ways in which we could improve the quality of our lives - for example, by valuing doctors above sports stars.
It all seems perfectly logical:

'Firstly... Secondly...'

In the body of the response, an alternative point of view is offered, but attacked in a number of ways. It is made to seem crazy ('ludicrous') and a series of rhetorical questions is intended to undermine it:

'How many goals do we remember? How many..?'

The repetition makes us imagine the writer shaking her head, as if she is amazed at people's behaviour...

GOOD POINTS:

- The response shows clear understanding of the structure: beginning, ending, and how it develops.
- Significant features are identified and illustrated.
- There is some personal response from the student ('it all seems...', 'it makes us imagine...').

◎ Language

There are two main ways in which you need to examine how language is used:

1. IS IT APPROPRIATE FOR THE AUDIENCE?

- An argument is unlikely to be successful if the audience is alienated by the language used or cannot understand it. For example:

  - Hey, guys, don't diss me

    is unlikely to impress middle-aged bank managers;

  - Those on the periphery of society should not be berated

    is unlikely to win the attention of the nation's young people.

- In a text, therefore, it is usually possible to identify elements of language which are aimed at the intended reader.

INTERVIEW

Hey, guys, too many questions!

2. HOW HAS THE LANGUAGE BEEN USED TO ENLIVEN THE TEXT?

If the language is boring, the text will not be successful, so writers use a range of strategies to entertain and interest the reader. Revision Session 3 will remind you of many language uses; others are involved in the following techniques for building an argument.

◎ Techniques

SCHOOL
OF
RHETORICAL
QUESTIONS.

Now why on earth would I want to go there?

- Your analysis will be more convincing if you can identify the techniques (or devices) a writer has employed to convince the reader and build the argument. Look out for:

  - rhetoric
    Language used for effect, such as:

    – rhetorical questions, which do not expect a reply:
    Don't we know this is lunacy? Is there nothing we can do?

    – exaggeration:
    There must be millions of rats just praying this law is passed and the sewers remain uncleaned...

  - examples
    Details selected to support a point:

    The same argument was put forward by admirals before the greatest maritime disaster...

  - anecdotes
    Brief stories used to show what happens, or what happened:

    Only last week, I was approached by a homeless person on my own street. She was not begging, however. She explained to me that...

  - quotations
    These will come from people with particular knowledge of the subject:

    'I can say that, in my role as mayor, I see what happens and know what is wrong...'

  - contrasts
    Writers will select details to juxtapose – to set beside each other – in order to clarify or justify their viewpoint:

    On one side, there are the rich, arguing for lower taxes. On the other side, sit the poor, who know that more money has to be raised to protect the health service.

  - humour
    This will be intended to encourage the reader to agree with the writer's opinion. There might be:

    – sarcasm:
    This is the greatest victory since Waterton Road Under 7s trounced Snapethorpe in the Lupset Women's Group's Minor Footie League in 1959.

- irony

This is when we find something amusing because of something else we know or because of something else that happens:

> He threw himself under a bus. If only he had bothered to check his lottery ticket...

⚡ A* EXTRA

▶ To gain a top grade, you need to analyse fully how these techniques have been used and comment carefully on their effectiveness. Your answer should include an exploration of a variety of ideas.

? CHECK YOURSELF QUESTION

Q What does the writer of this magazine article have to say about growing older and what techniques does he use to build his argument?

Age is a state of mind and I always knew that when Top of the Pops lost its interest I would be old. I was brought up on a Thursday evening fix of the latest sounds, but somehow I left it behind. And I suddenly realised I hadn't seen the show for years. It was time to take a fresh look and re-establish my credentials.

Shock and dismay. They had changed the day and instead of some friendly, reliable old DJ fronting the show, there was a half-naked girl who looked as if she should be in school, not devastating my blood pressure.

'Is she always on?' I asked my son, aghast.
'Chill, dad. Sometimes.'
'She just giggles and screams. And she's wearing underwear.'
'So? Don't we all?'

Then, the performers.

'Why do they do that?'
'What?'
'The rappers... Their hands... Why do they do that with their hands? No drier in the toilets?'
'It's what they do.'
'But why?'

You're old when you can't accept it's just what they do; when you stare, stunned, at the screen whilst your adolescent reads his Beano ('Do you ever read books?') without batting an eyelid, even though Christina Aguilera is on; and when you turn into your grandmother, sucking mints and looking forward to escaping and going to bed. To sleep.

It's weird when a whole part of your life has passed you by, but, frankly, you don't care because you are happier with your memories of Tony Blackburn and the Beatles and the Eurovision Song Contest and singers who had hair and sang and didn't have bodies with rings all over, like chain mail.

Of course, it's next stop afternoon bingo. Then a stair lift. And, frighteningly, what comes after that..?

It doesn't do to think too long. You are really, really old when the mint is actually sucked away. That way lies madness and darkness, when even Tony Blackburn doesn't matter any more.

Maybe I'll breathe deeply and try to appreciate Christina and the rappers. While I still can.

Answer is on page 146.

Language

Section A of Paper 1 will ask you to write about the language used in one or two of the unseen texts.

It is unwise to attempt to write about a whole text. You do not have enough time. It is better to write a lot about a little, rather than a little about a lot. Locate the most obvious linguistic features and concentrate on those. You might choose to deal with:
- sentences and paragraphs
- significant vocabulary
- punctuation
- similes, metaphors and other linguistic devices
- the style of the language.

◎ Sentences and paragraphs

■ The length of sentences and paragraphs, and the way they are constructed, can vary enormously and produce different effects.

For example, notice how:

● short sentences sometimes suggest speed or excitement:

> He ran forward. The ball fell at his feet. He shot.

or can indicate surprise or despair:

> Her inspiration stopped. Her career ended.

● long sentences can indicate calm:

> The sergeant reported that right along the river teams of men and women were resting at last and preparing to return to the headquarters for a much-needed rest.

or build to a climax:

> The crowds gasped as the top of the mountain blew away, clouds of ash shot hundreds of feet into the sky and rivers of lava, terrifying in the early dawn, shot upwards, then cascaded down into the valley.

■ Paragraphs, too, can create different effects. A very short paragraph, for instance, attracts attention, so that stress falls on the content. Tabloid newspaper articles are likely to have shorter paragraphs and contain less detail so that they can be read more easily. Broadsheet newspaper articles may have longer paragraphs containing more detail and analysis.

◎ Significant vocabulary

■ The sorts of words used in texts can also tell you a lot about the purpose of the text:

● Imperative verbs such as 'follow' and 'begin' suggest instructional writing.

● Connectives like 'since' and 'because' may indicate explanatory writing.

● Words such as 'however', 'nevertheless', and 'indeed' may come from persuasive or argumentative writing.

- The vocabulary can also tell you about the audience for a text:
  - Longer words suggest a text is aimed at an intelligent readership.
  - A text containing modern vocabulary, for instance dealing with ICT and communications, could be targeting younger people or those in the industry.
  - A text containing slang or colloquial terms might be aimed at teenagers.
  - Vocabulary associated with a specific subject would be used in an article aimed at experts, and so on.

Punctuation

- The punctuation of texts can clearly indicate the writer's intent, as in these headlines:

  1. **Teenager 'tortured to death'**

     The inverted commas indicate it may not have happened but show that someone has offered that opinion – or suggested it as a fact.

  2. **Let's focus on… improving your home**

     The ellipsis (…) suggests a surprise or that there are many things we could do. On another occasion, the ellipsis could suggest a fading away.

  3. **Holly hits out!!**

     The 'incorrect' double exclamation mark is to attract attention, suggest excitement or even surprise.

Similes, metaphors and linguistic devices

- Most candidates are able to write about **similes**, metaphors, **alliteration** and **onomatopoeia** when dealing with poetry on Paper 2, but many fail to realise that the same devices are used in non-fiction texts. This extract from an autobiography includes examples of all of them.

> They held us in a small room. We felt like — similes
> condemned men and smelt like battery hens. We had
> no idea of the day or the time and dreaded the dull — alliteration
> echoes of sharp boots and the crank of the lock on
> the door. — onomatopoeia
>
> They heralded the beginning of another eternity of — metaphor
> torture…

This is how one student analysed the use of language in that extract ...

> The writer makes their captivity vivid by using a series of linguistic devices. First, two similes stress their desperate situation ('like condemned men') and the inhuman conditions in which they were kept ('smelt like battery hens'). Deadly 'd's introduce the alliteration as their jailers approach - 'dreaded the dull...' - and then there is onomatopoeia which captures the sound as the key turns and their horrors are about to begin again: 'crank'. The primitive sound helps us understand their situation. Finally, there are metaphors: 'sharp boots', which suggests the violence they might face; and 'eternity of torture', which is how long and painful it must have seemed to them at the time.

GOOD POINTS:

- The analysis focuses on precise aspects of language, rather than generalising.
- Linguistic devices are discussed, not just identified.
- There is an awareness of the way the effects are linked and create an overall impression.

◎ Style

■ A text may be formal and written in standard English, or informal if the audience would respond more readily to that style (as in some letters, advertisements and articles).

You need to start by identifying the essential features of each. For example, if you were asked to compare a formal and an informal text, you might write:

> The first text is formal, using sentences like 'The government has taken a stance which...' while the second text is less formal and targets drug users: 'Get real...'

■ Then you need to look at the different techniques used. You may come across texts which persuade, argue, advise, inform, explain, describe, review or analyse and use a variety of techniques. For instance:

- **rhetoric** – language used for effect; in particular, note rhetorical questions:

  > Can this be acceptable?

- **emotive language** – touching the emotions:

  > They are tiny and cold and they are starving.

- **irony** (subtle mockery):

  > I have always thought it is a good idea to make the poor starve...

- **exaggeration**:

  > The Royal Family eats nothing but caviar for breakfast.

- **contrasts**:

  > The seabirds sing, while the fishermen starve.

⚡ **A* EXTRA**

▸ Practise finding and analysing these features in texts. Knowing how they can be used may have a considerable impact on your mark in your exam. So get into the habit of noticing what effect these features have on you when you meet them in your reading, and analyse how the writer has produced that response.

- **colloquial language** – as if people are chatting:

  If you want to pull, you have to impress the lads.

- **ambiguity** – where there can be more than one interpretation:

  Bird watching is a really exciting hobby.

- **inferences** – where things are suggested rather than clearly stated:

  He met the girl of his dreams. He didn't come home that night.

- **examples and quotations** – giving credibility to what is written

- **humour**

- **lists** – for emphasis.

■ The following extract from a newspaper article is short, but uses several of the above techniques.

> Who can fail to notice the Prime Minister's excellent track record when it comes to improving all areas of British life?
>
> We all recognise that approach which claims 'I'm a man o' the people', and don't the people just love him? Especially those paying taxes they can't afford, waiting in traffic that never moves, facing ever-mounting debt and an impoverished old age…

This is what one student wrote about the style of the extract …

The writer begins with apparent irony. The rhetorical question asks the reader to consider the PM's record, and suggests the track record may not be so good. Later, there is the implication that the people might not actually love him, while the colloquial 'I'm a man o' the people' might be poking fun at him, implying that his 'approach' is a pretence which 'we all recognise'.

Then there is a list of problems, which form a critical commentary on the government. It uses emotive detail ('they can't afford') and exaggeration ('traffic that never moves') as it moves to a cutting climax, with the elderly 'facing… an impoverished old age.'

GOOD POINTS:

- Language is analysed to explain the style.
- The writer's point of view is interpreted through the detail.
- Quotation is used to prove the points being made.

Q This comes from *Take a Break* magazine:

Gaze and laze

Take a break where the sun always shines

All eyes turn to the sea on this 30-mile stretch of Italy's western shore, considered one of the most beautiful coastlines in the world, where Campania gazes out into the Tyrrhenian reaches of the Mediterranean.

It takes in Sorrento, Positano, Salerno and Amalfi — which gives it the local name *Costiera Amalfitana* — and even extends into the sea.

Sitting off the coast like a satellite at the end of the peninsula, the island of Capri is just a 20-minute cruise away from Sorrento. From the port of Marina Grande it's a short ride by funicular railway to the labyrinth of narrow alleyways that make up Capri town.

But it is at Anacapri, the island's second town, that you'll find Capri's very own Garden of Eden, where mythological statues sit like sentinels surveying the deep blue waters. Or where classically draped figures from Italy's past appear to hold command over clouds fleeing across the contrasting blue of the sky.

Capri is blessed with virtually constant sunshine and many people over the ages have sought to stake a claim on this breathtaking corner of paradise. For some it may be a small but treasured apartment like the one in the picture, perhaps used as a regular retreat, or just rented for a couple of precious weeks in the year.

But others grand islan anir onc En ou h f

- What is the text's purpose and audience?

- How is language used by the writer?

- Is the language used successfully?

Answers is on page 147.

Layout and presentational devices

Paper 1 Section A will test your understanding of how layout and presentational devices are used in media texts. You will be expected to write about what the writer was hoping to achieve, and how:

- particular devices have been used, such as pictures, headlines and so on
- the presentation supports the writer's purpose.

Media language

- You will receive extra credit if you can use the correct media terms for presentational features. This does not mean you need specialist knowledge; there are fairly commonplace terms which will improve the quality of your performance.

- Layout means the way the page is arranged. Presentational devices are the individual features that are used to create the layout. When you are analysing the devices, it helps if you can use words like:

  - **headline**
  - **strapline**: a second, introductory headline, below the main one
  - **byline**: the name of the reporter, often stated clearly at the start of the report
  - **caption**: text under a photograph or diagram which explains it
  - **text box**
  - **columns**
  - **standfirst**: the introductory paragraph in an article or report, which could be in bold print or with the first word capitalised
  - **slogan**: a memorable word or phrase, designed to create interest
  - **pull-quote**: a quotation which is lifted from the article and set apart, perhaps in a bold type
  - **logos**: emblems to represent a product or company
  - **sub-headings**: which say what the next section of text is about and separate the text into smaller sections
  - **cross-heads**: sub-headings in the body of the text, and usually centred.

Examining how devices have been used

- If you just describe what is on the page, you are working at a very simple level. Instead, you should aim to say why the text has been designed in a particular way – what effect the writer is hoping to achieve.

- The following article uses a range of presentational devices.

gives perspective on article to follow: coloured box attracts attention to important point

caption focuses on Christina and her campaign

inset article indicates story/campaign has had publicity before

headline in midst of text – a quotation from Christina which stands out

strapline gives considerable detail

picture shows Daniel happy/ part of loving family

importance of campaign registered by mention of MP, using bold font

Christina's true story

There was no doubt about it – it was Daniel's signature all right. It hurt terribly just to see his handwriting. My son had only been dead for a few days – the ink had barely had time to dry.

The two officers from the Environmental Health department standing in my lounge had put it bluntly: "There's no minimum age for lip piercings, which means there really is very little we can do to prosecute the studio involved."

I couldn't believe what I was hearing. By law, these places weren't required to be registered.

Daniel died on 21 December 2002 – the same day as his brother Joseph's seventh birthday. I had cradled one son in my arms as he died and hours later was trying to console another on what should have been a day of celebration.

Like so many other 17-year-olds, Daniel had had his lip pierced. Within days of having the piercing, Daniel felt ill. He'd stopped eating and couldn't even get out of bed. When we saw a doctor, he suggested it was gastroenteritis. But I knew that it was more serious than that.

Daniel had had a heart condition since birth and I didn't want to take any chances. After seeing another GP, he was admitted to intensive care at Sheffield's Northern General Hospital and then to a coronary-care unit at Papworth Hospital.

The doctors had told us that a heart transplant might save Daniel, but he was too weak for surgery and spent those last ghastly days just

Christina has worked hard to create Dan Aid and to get the law on body piercing changed

Good life
My son died after having his lip pierced

It's too late for Daniel – but I've saved other teenagers' lives

Daniel Anderson was just 17 when he died from blood poisoning after having his lip pierced. His heartbroken mum Christina told *best* how she was determined to get the law changed to stop anything like this from happening again – now she's won her fight

getting weaker and weaker. It was absolutely heartbreaking, but the doctors said there was nothing they could do. And so Daniel died.

I vowed that some good should come from Daniel's tragic death. I owed it to other potential body-piercing victims to warn them of the lethal dangers of going to certain piercing parlours.

When Environmental Health asked me to verify Daniel's signature on the consent form he'd been given by the piercing studio, I felt sick and angry. My son had died in my arms, but they were telling me there was nothing they could do to prevent such a tragedy happening again. As the law stood, anyone could set up such a business without a licence or proper training. The only piercing you need a licence for is ears. It was crazy.

Then I remembered the tears of Daniel's elder brother Chris. "Daniel did nothing wrong," he'd cried. "All he did was get his lip pierced." That was when I decided I was going to make a difference.

After the officers left, I contacted my local MP, Meg Munn, and told her the story. She agreed to meet me, and I was relieved to find that she was very sympathetic.

Word must have got out about my crusade, as mums started stopping me in the playground at school to offer their support. "If I hear of any other children who've had bad experiences, I'll let you know," they promised. And they did.

Things snowballed and I needed to put all the information on a computer. I used the one I'd bought Daniel to help him with his homework.

My determination to ensure my son had not died in vain took over my life. I'm divorced and still had five other kids to think about: Chris, 22, William, 12, George, 10, Joseph, nine, and Nicole,

seven. Chris was a rock. He fed and bathed his brothers and sisters and made sure they got to bed on time with all their homework done.

On 27 February last year, Meg Munn tabled a debate in the House of Commons on the laws surrounding piercing studios. The campaign was getting recognition. Daniel wouldn't be forgotten.

Sometimes the strain did get to me. Even with Chris's aid, there were times when I had to go to my bedroom and cry. But I made sure it was when the kids were at school or asleep. I had to be strong for them. I thank Daniel for giving me that strength. He'd fought against the infection that finally took his life. I couldn't let him down.

"They've done it!" Meg shouted down the phone last February – MPs had voted to change the law to force piercing parlours to be registered. It meant anyone who didn't have trained staff and sterile facilities could be closed down. I was overjoyed, laughing and crying at the same time. Our Dan Aid campaign had done so much.

Now I'm doing workshops in local schools to explain the safety issues involved with piercing and, with more funding, I hope to produce leaflets for all schools, youth clubs and colleges in the UK.

I wouldn't want any mum to go through what I did. With this campaign, they won't have to.
As told to Adrian Troughton

MP Meg Munn (Labour MP for Sheffield Heeley) says "Christina is an amazing person and deserves her success. That the law has been changed is due, in a massive part, to her campaign."
■ For more information, visit *www.danaid.com*

Daniel pictured with his younger sister Nicole

36 *best*

Christina and Daniel are clearly the centre of the article. Christina's picture, like her campaign, dominates the page and is linked by colour to the box at the top and the headline. Immediately, we see that she is Christina, her story is true and we know that they are her words in the headline. 'Dan Aid' is also made significant - on her T shirt as publicity and on the computer, to show the campaign has extended to the internet. It needs to stand out because it is the most important part of the article.

The small 'Good life' article has blue as its dominant colour, bright and cheerful, and that is reflected in the 'Dan Aid' logo, suggesting that Daniel had a good life. The picture of Daniel makes him seem loving (cheek to cheek with his sister); and the 'everyday' picture of the pierced lip shows the reader how something so 'normal' can have far-reaching consequences. The strapline offers important information, in bold, to attract readers by giving the main details of the story; and the mention of the MP in bold at the end adds credibility to Christina's campaign...

Linking presentation with the writer's purpose

- Presentational devices are used to further the writer's purpose. For example, the writer will be hoping to stress a particular aspect of a story or emphasise a particular quality of a product.

- Look carefully at this article and the student's comment below.

Britain gives £6m to help fight Aids

BY JAYNE ATHERTON

BRITAIN is to pay an extra £3 million a year towards fighting the global spread of Aids, it emerged yesterday.

Ministers marked World Aids Day by announcing they would double a donation to the United Nations effort to tackle HIV and Aids to £6 million.

They called on other countries to step up efforts to fight the epidemic, which has infected 60 million people and killed 20 million.

International Development Secretary Hilary Benn said it was crucial to help developing countries develop drug programmes.

Young Aids patients queue for lunch at a children's home in Bangkok

He said Britain would also work with the World Health Organisation to ensure 6million people received the latest anti-retroviral treatments.

Britain is the second-largest donor in the fight against Aids, giving £270 million a year for work in 40 countries.

The headline is presenting Britain's contribution positively. The caption sets the picture in a context (the Aids payment is destined for relief operations overseas - and, here, the implication is it will help children). The coloured picture makes the children look attractive but desperate and shows them having to wait in line, as if they have no choice but to queue for vital supplies.

■ Now, a rather different article, from the *Daily Mail*. Again, look carefully at the layout and presentational devices. What do you think the purpose of the article might be?

Families to spend less on gifts at Christmas

By Consumer Affairs Correspondent

Families are ready to begin tightening their belts this Christmas over repeated warnings over personal debt soaring.

Shoppers will spend an average £16 less on presents – around £345 compared to £362 last year – according to a survey.

The total spent by each person during the festive season on gifts, food, drink, and cards is about £868, says the Switch debit card group.

On average, we buy gifts for 12 friends and family members. And while parents will be keeping a scrooge-like watch on their spending this year, sacrifices will be made to ensure presents are lavished on children, reveals the report.

'Scots ready for a spree'

Some 35 per cent of those surveyed said their most expensive purchase would be for a child with an average

THE COST OF CELEBRATING		
Item	2002	2003
Most expensive present	£108	£123
Other presents	£254	£223
Cards, postage	£18	£17
Decorations, etc	£23	£30
Food	£107	£115
Drink	£60	£64
Other items*	£298	£290
Total	£868	£862

*Pantomimes, parties, new clothes etc

In fact, Scotland is preparing for the biggest festive spree in the UK.

Total spending per head north of the border is put at £1,040 compared to

The study suggests more people are looking to the Continent for Christmas bargains. Around 23 per cent said they planned to do some shopping abroad,

---

Here is one student's answer ...

✓ The headline gives a clear message, and at first glance the picture would seem to be saying that Christmas will still be happy: mother and son are smiling and seem content. However, the spending chart indicates just how expensive Christmas is, including its darkened heading, with its stress on 'cost', which is mirrored by the darkened totals at the bottom. The numbers stand out, and appear high. The pull-quote 'Scots ready for a spree' also seems to contradict the headline. The by-line 'Consumer Affairs Correspondent' gives the article some credibility, but without reading the piece, it is impossible to say where the emphasis will lie. The presentation, therefore, is confusing and not altogether successful.

GOOD POINTS:
- The different features are analysed.
- The candidate evaluates the text's success and offers criticism, supported by textual references.

⚡ ***A* EXTRA***

▸ Successfully evaluating the *effectiveness* of the presentational devices used is a high order skill which will be rewarded with a high mark.
▸ You need to be able to develop comments on each device in detail.

Q What impression of Nivea for Men is this advertisement trying to create?

Explain the use of layout and presentational devices.

Answer is on page 147.

Selecting and using textual references

To support the points you make in Section A responses, you need to refer directly to the text to prove your points. You must:

- select references which are suitable for the task
- use the references appropriately: quote briefly and explain the effects.

◎ Selecting references

■ To find essential details or quotations, make sure you read the question carefully to see exactly what is required. Notice helpful information, such as:

'Read the opening paragraph and explain...'

'Find three facts and say how they support what the writer believes...'

'What techniques are used to convince the reader that...'

■ Having decided what is needed, express your ideas clearly. Remember that irrelevant references will not improve your mark.

◎ Using textual references

■ The purpose of making a textual reference is to show the examiner that you have read the text carefully and that any ideas you are putting forward arise from the text itself. In other words, you are engaging with the material, rather than just offering random thoughts.

> When she addressed the conference, Cecily Bowers was quite clear about what her objectives would be. She felt that in just two years' time, people would notice the difference; there would be the beginning of works to transform the environment, and even the quality of water would be improved ...
>
> From *The Parish Magazine*

Look at this response to the extract:

The writer makes Ms Bowers seem confident from the start. He says she:
'was clear about what her objectives would be'.
The 'clarity' suggests she has thought through her ideas, and can put them across forcibly.

Then, he goes on to indicate some of the improvements she is intending, including the water quality in the district. Since there is no hint of cynicism, these details are, presumably, included to illustrate what is likely to happen.

⚡ A* EXTRA

▶ Make sure quotations are always clear. Put *inverted commas* around any words you quote and *indent* longer quotations. Take care to set short quotations into fluent sentences, and always make at least one comment on each quotation you present to explain why you have included it.

⚡ A* EXTRA

▶ Examiners always reward the *development* of ideas. Try to:
  - explain *what* the material is saying, *why* and *how*
  - link the reference you have selected to the rest of the text by placing it in context and analysing its significance.
▶ Top candidates can see the inter-connectedness of the text, and can cross-reference their comments to construct an imaginative and personal response.

GOOD POINTS:

- The candidate has used a textual reference to support each point. In one case this is a quotation, in the other a textual detail.
- The significance of the textual references is explained.

Q This is part of an advertising feature for MüllerPuds. How does the writer try to attract women to the product? Use textual references to support your answer.

ADVERTISEMENT FEATURE

Don't want to spend half a day preparing your fave puds? Then let someone else do it for you...

Pudding is served!

Your favourite pud *in seconds!*

Invited the girls round to catch up on the gossip? Take the phone off the hook. Put the kettle on.

All you need now is some scrummy comfort food.

What better way to round off a girls' night-in this winter than with some classic puddings just like Mum would make?

Sticky Toffee, Jam or Golden Syrup-drenched Sponge Pudding covered in real dairy custard... *Mmm...*

Or delicious Rhubarb or Apple Crumble smothered with custard, too.

Sounds too much like hard work – slaving over a hot stove and missing out on all the fun?

Well now you don't have to! Let Müller make them for you, and you can treat your mates to a selection of their all-time favourite puddings.

Choose scrummy crumble or succulent sponge, all served with creamy custard, straight from the fridge or warmed up in the microwave

Just like Mum used to make

in just 60 seconds!

There – what could be easier? And what could be tastier? Definitely worth staying in for!

Thanks to Müller Puds, you can now treat your mates, your kids – even your man if he decides to stay in, too! – to their very own favourite pud, perfectly cooked every time.

Whatever the time of day, Müller Puds capture the classic taste of childhood perfectly. As reassuringly warming as

your own mum's cooking, and with the great taste you know you'll get from Müller. They're just right for slipping into a packed-lunch box and ideal when friends drop by.

With Müller Puds you can treat yourself and your family to your all-time favourite classic combo for just 59p. With five delicious puddings, there's something for everyone – Apple or Rhubarb Custard & Crumble, or Jam, Golden Syrup and Sticky Toffee Custard & Sponge.

What could be easier? The only problem is which one to choose...

For more info, check out the refrigerated section at your local store or log onto www.muller.co.uk

müller **loue**

müllerPuds

Müller and Puds are registered trademarks. Photos: Richard Kendal

Answer is on page 148.

Analysing text types

There are a number of different **text types** within media and non–fiction (see page 2). Each is targeted at a particular **audience** and is written for a particular **purpose**.

Each text type uses particular devices – in language, layout and presentational features – to achieve its purpose and to reach its audience effectively.

To be successful in your exam, you need to recognise what the writer is wishing to achieve and the methods used. This demands a careful reading of the text.

I'm certainly not buying one of these- it promises to make me lose 10lb in a week!

◎ News reports

This is a news report from *The Sun*. The annotations make clear for you which devices have been used.

headline

'Protest' gives immediate impression

strapline

mention of 'crowds' not evident in picture – stress on environmental impact again

alliteration 'toxic time bomb' gives ticking effect

emotive language makes ship sound dangerous

'TOXIC' RUST-BUCKET IS HERE

Protest as ship docks

A RUSTING ghost ship dubbed a "toxic time bomb" arrives in Britain yesterday — to be greeted by crowds of angry environmental protesters.

The Caloosahatchee, one of four redundant US Navy vessels being sent here to be scrapped, docked at Hartlepool, Teesside.

Protesters say they are packed with toxic chemicals and must be returned to America.

The Government allowed the ships to dock in Hartlepool — but says the local firm that won the contract to scrap them must not start until a legal row over their fate is decided.

Protester Barbara Crosbie, 36, from Hartlepool said yesterday: "Ninety per cent of people living here don't think this is right. We're angry and want all these ships sent back."

short paragraphs give 'punchy' **tabloid** effect

text box to make report stand out

factual details set out

final word given to protester, for impact

grey-fill for dismal effect

picture: ship appears old/ready to scrap and needs tug

people look cold; photographers evident, so a media event; one man waving – or shaking fist

This is how one student chose to analyse how effective the text is …

The report comes from a tabloid newspaper and is against the arrival of the ship. The way it is presented, looking grey, grim and dangerous, and the way a metaphor is used to describe it ('a rusting ghost ship'), make the reader feel immediately that this is undesirable.

Because the report is so short, with just one sentence in each paragraph, we immediately think it is set out for anyone to read. A broadsheet newspaper would have gone into much more detail. This is simple reporting for those with little time or who would not be interested in more complex details…

GOOD POINTS:

- Both presentation and language are used to explain the purpose and audience.
- Precise details from the text are used as evidence.

◎ Web pages

Web pages have different features and devices, which are used for different purposes. Again, the annotations make this clear for you.

colours to attract attention: deep blue suggests heat, green offers shade, wide beaches apparent

solving dilemmas over choice; sounds exciting

links provided

for further searches

website provider indicated

indication of content

range of content for readers

logo stands out

range of linked topics

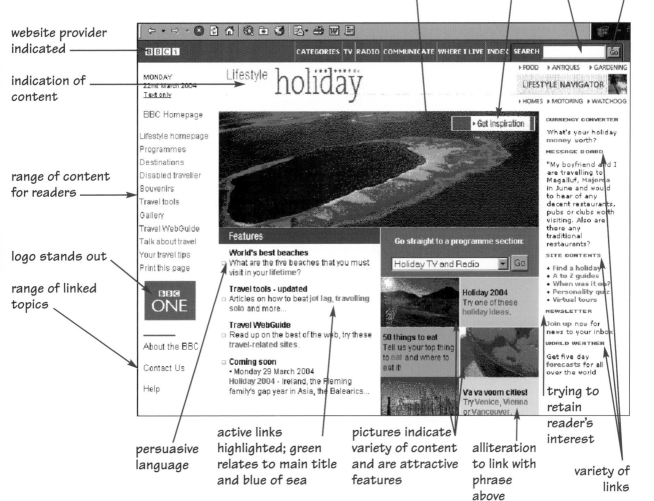

persuasive language

active links highlighted; green relates to main title and blue of sea

pictures indicate variety of content and are attractive features

alliteration to link with phrase above

trying to retain reader's interest

variety of links

Asked to analyse the web page, one student began like this:

This is a successful web page, designed to interest those considering a holiday and tempt those who had not previously considered taking one. The main picture looks breathtaking and will attract any potential traveller; the smaller pictures are varied and make us want to travel (there is the romance of the sunset, the succulence of the fruit and the beauty of Venice). The text also demands attention: there are the imperatives – 'Try…', 'Tell us…', – and a range of associated topics, all clearly highlighted. For instance, many words are written in blue to stand out but also to link with the main title and the tempting blue of the sea. A sense of humour and modernity is introduced, with the reference to the car advertisement ('Va va voom cities'), and even the punctuation is used effectively: ellipses to suggest there is so much more to follow and exclamation marks to emphasise the excitement of it all…

GOOD POINTS:

- The candidate has dealt with purpose and audience.
- Precise details from the text are referred to.
- The details are considered critically, to analyse the text's success.
- Both presentation and language are analysed.

◉ Autobiographies

■ This extract is from an autobiography by Sir Robin Day. Sir Robin used to interview politicians on television, and this is about his first ever time in front of the cameras – in the 1950s, when television was not so technical and there were no autocues!

■ There are no presentational devices used in a text of this sort, so the focus is on the language.

short, dramatic first sentence

detail brings scene to life

tension builds

fear that material is not good enough: threat of disaster

countdown moves text towards the climax

short, dramatic ending

'I was ready to go. But there was a little more delay. The lighting was causing trouble with my spectacles – reflection flashes from the lenses and shadows from the heavy hornrims. An engineer climbed up ladders to adjust the arc-lamps until the director in the control room was satisfied. It seemed to take a very long time. I began to sweat under the heat of the lights.

We had been asked to memorise our material so that we would not have to look down. They wanted to see us looking full-face into the camera. I took a final look at my notes. The phrases which last night were crisp and bright seemed limp and dull, but it was too late to make any changes.
'Are you ready?' called the floor manager. I nodded.
'Stand by.' He stood to one side of the camera, and raised his arm above his shoulder.
'Thirty seconds to go…. Fifteen seconds.'
Suddenly the floor-manager jabbed his hand down towards me. A red light glowed on top of the camera. This was it.'

Look at this extract from an analysis of the text:

The text sets out to illustrate to Robin Day's fans just what he had to cope with. It begins with a short sentence and ends the same way. It seems tense, as if Sir Robin is taking short breaths...

The problems with the glasses and the lights are mentioned to show how everything seems to be going wrong, making Sir Robin more worried ('I began to sweat...'). Obviously, it is all building up inside him, so he seems very human and doubts even the quality of his material:

'The phrases... seemed limp and dull'...

GOOD POINTS:
- The whole of the text is examined.
- Relevant quotations are used to support the student's ideas.

? CHECK YOURSELF QUESTION

Q What is the purpose and audience for this advertisement and how does it achieve its effects?

Yours to spend: 10,000 Euro!

Enjoy unique benefits when you shop in Vienna during the "shop & win" campaign in January and February 2004. Plus: you can even win a shopping spree worth 10,000 Euro. From hip shopping mile to nostalgic old-city shop – Vienna offers a choice of 20,000 stores.

shop & win

BOOK NOW!
3 days "Vienna Joie de Vivre"
2 nights B&B, 4* hotel Vienna Card, Albertina admission, from £ 75

WIEN-HOTELS & INFO
TEL. 0043-1-24 555
www.vienna.info

Vienna
Wien · Vienne · 維也納 · ウィーン

waits for you

Answer is on page 148.

Comparing texts

One question on Section A of Paper 1 will expect you to compare two texts. This could be a simple comparison, for example asking you to compare the writers' use of language. However, it is more likely that you will have to write about a number of features in the texts, such as layout, language and argument.

You will have to:
- provide the right details
- make all cross-references clear.

◎ Providing the right details

■ Your first priority is to ensure you are providing the information that is required. If you are presented with a stem question followed by bullets, this will mean:
  - responding to the stem
  - applying the stem to each bullet in turn.

For example, you might get a question like:

Which text is the more successful?————————→ stem
Compare the texts by writing about how the writers have used:
- fact and opinion ⎤
- argument   ⎬————————→ bullets
- presentational devices. ⎦

■ In this case, you would be looking at how *successfully* the writers have used fact and opinion, argument and presentational devices. Your mark would be reduced if you analysed the features but did not evaluate their success and say *which works better, and why*.

◎ Making clear cross-references

■ The vital element in answering such questions well is that you should *compare* the texts. It is not enough to write an analysis of one, then an analysis of the other. In making references to the texts, you must clearly link one text to the other. Notice how the second answer below does this successfully, while the first one simply refers to the two texts in turn:

The first text concentrates on giving advice to old people and uses lots of facts and figures. The second text encourages relatives to invest in security for senior citizens.

The first text concentrates on giving advice to old people. However, the second text ...

■ It is useful to have a stock of words and phrases to make comparisons clear, such as:

similarly   in contrast   Just as...   so...   whereas

    on the other hand   but   While the first text..., the second text

    in comparison   The second text, though...

◎ Two texts to compare

■ Read the texts below, then look at the annotated student's answer to this question:

> Compare these texts by saying whether they will appeal to their audience.
>
> Write about the writers' use of:
> • fact and opinion
> • language.

■ **Text 1**
This is from an obituary for the poet Charles Causley (an account, straight after his death, of his main achievements) in *The TES*, a teachers' newspaper:

■ **Text 2**
This newspaper article offers a different view of young people:

At Launceton voluntary primary he discovered by accident the power of the ballad – a form he later made his own – to quell unruly eight and nine-year-olds.

In a TES interview to celebrate his 70th birthday, he told Neil Philip: 'I used to have a double class of boys every Thursday afternoon. There were 50 or 60 of them, quite a horror, and I had the wrong books with me. At the top of the pile I had a selection of English and Scottish ballads ... I opened it in desperation ... Stop a riot with a ballad.'

The boys were transfixed, but Mr Causley never forced poetry on anyone. He simply made it a natural part of the school day.

A pensioner's life has been made a misery by 'young vandals and thugs'.

Frank Blackburn, 78, who lives on the Albany Estate, has been a prisoner in his house each evening for over a year. Groups of children, many as young as 7 or 8, have made him fear for his life and the safety of his property.

'They gather every night,' says Frank. 'The police don't do anything about it.'

Stones have been thrown through his windows, excrement has been pushed through his letter box and he cannot sleep. Gangs roam the area, shouting and drinking. Other older residents are just as fearful.

A police spokesman said they are currently dealing with the matter.

This is how an A* student responded:

The audiences for these texts are different. The piece on Charles Causley is written for teachers, and therefore presents a positive image of Causley in the teaching situation, whereas the other article is for a more general readership and concentrates on the pensioner's suffering, to get a sympathetic response.

The facts in the TES obituary show how difficult Causley's situation was ('50 or 60 of them'; 'I had the wrong books with me'). However, the wonder of what he achieved relies on his own opinion of what they were like. Originally the situation was 'quite a horror' but then 'The boys were transfixed'; the book of ballads was opened 'in desperation' but soon became 'a natural part of the school day'. We rely on Causley's interpretation for the final impression of how poetry managed to 'quell' the children.

Concentrates on the appeal to their intended audiences.

'whereas' links the texts

Focus on how facts and opinions are used in the obituary.

In contrast, the article's vision of young people seems much more immediate and believable. Facts and opinions are interwoven throughout, and we accept both as truth. The facts are grim: stones through the windows, and excrement; gangs 'shouting and drinking' and Frank fearing for his life. If the police 'are currently dealing' with it, that seems ineffective. What is worse, this is happening to a 78-year-old, persecuted by 7- or 8-year-olds. The opinions give a further impression of the children ('young vandals and thugs'), of the effects (his life is 'a misery', whilst the 'other older residents are just as fearful'), and of the police who 'don't do anything about it'.

The language is unpleasant: 'misery', 'thugs'. Frank is pictured as a metaphorical prisoner. This is an estate plagued by 'stones', 'excrement', 'gangs' and fear. The final, matter-of-fact statement from the police seems cold and unfeeling, making us sympathise with the old people even more.

However, in the Causley extract the language is different, and inspiring: 'he discovered... the power'. This is, after all, to 'celebrate' his birthday. He is made to seem heroic:
   'Stop a riot with a ballad',
and an example to others, since the boys were 'transfixed'. The language, though, seems exaggerated.

In fact, the image of Causley's children seems to come from a different age. They are 'unruly', which suggests just naughtiness, and they are not bad enough to require punishment. Teachers reading the obituary will feel admiration for him, but an ordinary reader might suspect his pupils were not evil if he found 50 or 60 of them easy to 'quell'. The ordinary reader, though, will recognise the images in the newspaper article and will be upset by them – which is what the writer intended.

'In contrast' makes a further clear comparison.

The focus here is on facts and opinions in the article.

Language comment ties in with and seems to grow from impression created in previous paragraph.

'However' and 'different' identify contrast.

Final paragraph summarises the impression created by the texts and returns to the stem of the question – the appeal to their intended audience – to conclude.

GOOD POINTS:
- All four elements of the question are dealt with (comparison, appeal to audience, use of fact and opinion and language).
- Analysis is thorough using precise quotations and comments on them, and apt cross-references.
- Effects are evaluated ('Teachers reading the obituary will feel admiration for him, but an ordinary reader might suspect...').
- There is personal response to the texts ('more immediate and believable', 'seems to come from a different age').
- There is full understanding of the texts and what the question demands.

Q   Read the texts below, then answer this question:

What impression of parenthood is created in these texts?
Compare:
- what the parents are like
- the writers' use of language.

Text 1

This is an extract from *Fatherhood*, a book in which American comedian Bill Cosby gives his thoughts on how parents and children develop together:

You see, the wives *pretend* to turn over the child-raising job to us fathers, but they don't really mean it. One day, my wife said to me, 'He's *your* child, I wash my hands of him.'

Where is this sink where you can wash your hands of a child? I want to wash my hands too, and then the boy can go free.

For someone who supposedly had washed her hands of the child, my wife still sounded unwashed to me.

'You go and talk to him right now.'
'I certainly will.'
'But the thing is, Bill, you always let him have his own way.'

'Look, you've washed your hands; he's not yours, he's mine. So let me handle it.'
'I want you to be hard on him.'

She was singing this song now; but three years before, when I had wanted to set him on fire, she'd said, 'Oh, *please* don't. He's such a little boy.'

And I had said, 'No, burn him now.'

Yes, amid all the love, there are still dark threats in any normal family, especially if a man and a woman have been reckless enough to allow the joy of making love to lead to something as dangerous as children.

Text 2

This is a letter sent to the Agony Aunt of a national newspaper:

Dear Jane,

I hope you can help me. I am desperate. I am a single parent who has to work, and I get no support of any kind from my ex-husband. I have been alone for over four years now and my two teenage daughters seem totally out of control. I am at my wits' end.

My eldest daughter is just sixteen and feels she can do exactly as she wants. When she goes out, I have no idea where she is; and she comes home when she feels like it. She uses the house like a hotel, but doesn't pay for her room or her board. I am a servant in my own home.

Her sister is fourteen and constantly in trouble at school. She has recently started truanting, and I'm now afraid I might be taken to court and sent to prison because of it. She treats me like dirt even when her friends are round, and she steals money from my purse.

I am close to giving up on them both, and feel suicidal. What can I do?

Answer is on page 149.

POETRY FROM DIFFERENT CULTURES AND TRADITIONS

What you will be assessed on

Paper 2, Section A, will expect you to compare two poems from different cultures and traditions. The poems will be taken from your Anthology.

There will be two questions, but you will only have to answer one of them.

In both questions, you will be asked about a named poem, and asked to compare it with another of your choice.

One question will target the first cluster of poems in the Anthology, the other question will target the second cluster.

You will be expected to spend 45 minutes on your response. This will count for 15% of your total mark for the exam.

◎ Responding to Poetry from Different Cultures and Traditions

■ In both questions, you will be expected to write about elements in the poems which show clearly that the poems come from different cultures.

■ You might, for example, be asked about the setting of the poems, or the situation of the individuals in the poems, or about poverty in the poems, or something similar. In each of these examples, you will automatically end up writing about the culture from which the poem comes, or which it concerns. You will, therefore, have fulfilled the 'different culture' requirement.

◎ The questions you will be asked

■ The questions that are set will be based upon the assessment criteria for Reading. Examiners will be assessing your ability to:

1. *Read, with insight and engagement, making appropriate references to texts and developing and sustaining interpretations of them*

    You will be expected to understand what the poets are saying, hopefully moving beyond the obvious meaning and examining the deeper messages the poets offer. In other words, you will range across the poems and deal with why they have been written. You should support your ideas with reference to and quotation from the poems.

    - See Sessions 1-5

2. *Select material appropriate to your purpose, collate material from different sources and make cross-references*

    References to the poems need to be relevant, so you need to focus on the question that is asked, avoid irrelevancies and select ideas and quotations that are apt. It is not enough simply to write about two poems; for top grades, you need to make clear comparisons of messages, poetic techniques or whatever is required by the question.

    - See Sessions 2-5

3. *Understand and evaluate how writers use linguistic, structural and presentational devices to achieve their effects, and comment on ways language varies and changes*

    You will be expected to show how the poets have used language, what effect it has and why the poets have used it in particular ways and for particular purposes. You will be writing about how the language is used appropriately to convey a particular message. If you can evaluate the usage – say how successful it is – you will be rewarded with a high mark. You will also need to consider other presentational elements such as the structure, including how it begins, develops and ends, as well as the way it is set out on the page.

    - See Sessions 3-5

Cultures and traditions

The questions on Paper 2 Section A will focus, in part, on the different cultures or traditions identifiable in the poems.

In some instances these will be suggested by the specific language that has been used, but the question could also ask about:
• people
• settings
• situations
• problems.

◉ Language

■ In some of the Anthology poems, language plays a significant role in setting the poem within a particular culture.

• It can show how people speak:

> munay hutoo kay aakhee jeebh aakhee bhasha
> (*from Search For My Tongue* by Sujata Bhatt)

> Explain yuself
> wha yu mean
> (*Half-Caste* by John Agard)

• Elsewhere, it gives us names: Oya, Shango and Hattie (*Hurricane Hits England*); or introduces items unfamiliar to many in Britain: yams in *Not My Business* and a salwar kameez in *Presents from my Aunts in Pakistan*.

• There are also very different situations:

> When peaceful clouds were reflected in the paddies
> and the water buffalo stepped surely along the terraces
> (*What Were They Like?* by Denise Levertov)

'Paddies' and 'terraces' give a clear sense of the different culture.

■ It is very important to show that you understand both how the poets use language, and why.

Look at this extract from a student's answer about the language used in *from Unrelated Incidents*.

---

thi reason

a talk wia

BBC accent

iz coz yi

widny wahnt

mi ti talk

aboot thi

trooth wia

voice lik

wanna yoo

scruff...

yooz doant no

thi trooth

yirsellz cawz

yi canny talk

right.

Extract: *from Unrelated Incidents*

In *from Unrelated Incidents*, Tom Leonard uses a regional voice to criticise BBC English and all it represents. We appreciate his accent and the pronunciation because it seems ordinary – and, arguably, more honest than the manufactured television version of 'trooth'. When the newsreader says we would not want him to talk 'lik wanna yoo scruff', we are presented with an image of Glasgow, peopled by ordinary folk; but we are left to wonder whether they are people that we would trust more than someone who uses 'received pronunciation'.

GOOD POINTS:
• The focus is upon how and why the language is used.
• The use of language is explained ('we are presented with...').
• There is a personal reaction to the language ('We appreciate his accent...').

People and settings

- In most of the poems, the people and the places where they live are different from those we would find in Britain.

  - In *What Were They Like?* by Denise Levertov, we have:

    > peasants; their life
    > was in rice and bamboo.

  - In *Two Scavengers in a Truck, Two Beautiful People in a Mercedes* by Lawrence Ferlinghetti, the American situation is closer to our own world, but still different:

    > a bright yellow garbage truck
    >   with two garbagemen in red plastic blazers
    >   standing on the back stoop...

Situations and problems

- The sense of coming from or being in a different cultural situation, and the problems which arise, are common themes running through the clusters.

  For example, in *Island Man* by Grace Nichols, the central character finds himself in a relatively alien environment. He has left his home, with its surf, seabirds and fishermen, and is now coping with life in a huge city. He has to drag himself out of bed to face its challenges:

  > island man heaves himself

  > Another London day

  The final line, separated, shows the significance of 'another London day', which seems heavy and depressing.

  Other poems show problems. In *Limbo* by Kamau Braithwaite, we are presented with the world of slavery and the suffering of the Africans. The plight of the slaves is desperate:

  > stick is the whip
  > and the dark deck is slavery

  though the ending suggests there might be salvation of some kind:

  > and the music is saving me.

  Often, though, there seem no solutions, so we are faced with 'the perpetuity of evil' (*Vultures* by Chinua Achebe) and told in Tatamkhula Afrika's poem that *Nothing's Changed*.

  In many instances, people just have to struggle on. In *Night of the Scorpion*, Nissim Ezekiel details her mother's suffering, then reveals her mother's reaction, which indicates that her only thoughts were for her children and, perhaps, makes us think that her whole life in the village has been a struggle and that she has become used to pains:

  > My mother only said
  > Thank God the scorpion picked on me
  > And spared my children.

A* EXTRA

- Since people and their environments are likely to be central to questions on this paper, revision of these features is particularly important.
- You might be presented with questions which begin:
  What impression of society is given in...
  or
  What problems does the poet highlight in... and how do the people react? Compare this situation with another from a poem of your choice.
  Thorough preparation for such tasks leads to more detailed responses and higher grades.

A* EXTRA

- Since people and their environments are likely to be central to questions on this paper, revision of these features is particularly important.
- You might be presented with questions which begin:
  What impression of society is given in...
  or
  What problems does the poet highlight in... and how do the people react? Compare this situation with another from a poem of your choice.
  Thorough preparation for such tasks leads to more detailed responses and higher grades.

At other times, there are some flashes of hope for the future, such as when Imtiaz Dharker conjures a positive vision and excitement:

This is the time and place
to be alive.   (This Room)

Also, Derek Walcott demonstrates how we can come to a peace within ourselves and how our lives will be richer because of our understanding:

You will love again the stranger who was yourself. (Love After
Love)

CHECK YOURSELF QUESTION

Q   It always helps to revise poems in pairs, since you will have to compare two poems in the exam itself. Consider the lists below. Decide which poems you would use to respond to the given themes, and why.

Cluster 1

Themes	Poems
Suffering	*Nothing's Changed*
Poverty	*Limbo*
Inequality	*Island Man*
Man and Nature	*Night of the Scorpion*
Contrasting cultures	*What Were They Like?*
	Two Scavengers in a Truck
	Blessing
	Vultures

Cluster 2

Themes	Poems
Living between cultures	*Love After Love*
Language problems	*from Unrelated Incidents*
Changes	*Presents from my Aunts in Pakistan*
Dealing with the unacceptable	*Hurricane Hits England*
A positive outlook	*Half-Caste*
	Not My Business
	from Search For My Tongue
	This Room

Answer is on page 150.

Content, attitude and message

When you write about poems from different cultures and traditions, the content of the poems may be a central feature of the question you are asked.

You may have to comment on:

- the content of the poems
- the poets' attitudes to the subject
- the messages in the poems.

◎ What the poem is saying

- For each of the poems you are studying, you need to understand exactly what the poem is saying. Without this basic knowledge, you cannot hope to write effectively in your exam.

  Look at these sample annotations on the opening of *Vultures* by Chinua Achebe:

In the greyness	
and drizzle of one despondent	depressing scene to link with topic
dawn unstirred by harbingers	
of sunbreak a vulture	vulture unaffected by daylight
perching high on broken	linked to images of deadness
bone of a dead tree	
nestled close to his	affectionate with mate
mate his smooth	
bashed-in head, a pebble	
on a stem rooted in	described in terms from nature
a dump of gross	
feathers, inclined affectionately	
to hers. Yesterday they picked	
the eyes of a swollen	gruesome details
corpse in a water-logged	
trench and ate the	
things in its bowel. Full	full, they roost
gorged they chose their roost	
keeping the hallowed remnant	corpse considered of religious importance
in easy range of cold	
telescopic eyes…	vultures' eyes unfeeling and sharp
Strange	
indeed how love in other	
ways so particular	generalisation about love and how creatures behave when in love
will pick a corner	
in that charnel-house	
tidy it and coil up there, perhaps	
even fall asleep – her face	love makes us ignore what might otherwise appal us
turned to the wall!	

This is how one student began to analyse Achebe's message...

The vultures of the title are described in some detail by the poet. They are a couple, part of nature ('a pebble on a stem') but unpleasant to look at, the male with a 'bashed-in head'. The 'cold telescopic' eyes are frightening and the atmosphere around them is similarly depressing. There is drizzle, no appreciation of sunbreak, and the situation is compared to a 'charnel house'.

This is because death is part of the description, for although the birds are lovers (he has his head 'inclined affectionately to hers'), they have gorged on a corpse, eating its eyes and what was in the bowel - grim details about a quite frightening pair.

The final section of the extract comments on how those in love can overlook unpleasantness in their proximity, metaphorically turning their face to the wall. They can live and cope in what is, in truth, a vile situation.

◎ The poet's attitude and message

1. *VULTURES* BY CHINUA ACHEBE

■ When poets describe situations, they present them in such a way that the reader is led to consider an underlying message. So, for example, in *Vultures* we are led to consider how acceptable it is both to feed on death and to love. The gruesome detail and the inclusion of the Commandant of Belsen might lead us to suppose the poet finds such behaviour extremely unpleasant.

■ The poet does, though, point out that even the worst offenders can show some 'tenderness'. In this case, the man in charge of the death camp is also a loving 'Daddy' who lavishes treats on his doting child.

	GOOD POINTS: ✓
	• The extract is considered in its entirety.
	• All the ideas are supported with precise textual detail.
	• There are three clear sections: the birds, their behaviour and the general point to conclude.

... Thus the Commandant at Belsen Camp going home for the day with fumes of human roast clinging rebelliously to his hairy nostrils will stop	man in charge of concentration camp: the worst of humanity?
	vivid, unpleasant image
at the wayside sweet-shop and pick up a chocolate for his tender offspring waiting at home for Daddy's return...	
	contrasting impression
Praise bounteous providence if you will that grants even an ogre a tiny glow-worm	evil and affection brought together
tenderness encapsulated in icy caverns of a cruel heart or else despair	tenderness balanced against coldness
for in the very germ of that kindred love is lodged the perpetuity of evil.	there is love, but the love leads to a continuation of the evil

2. NOT MY BUSINESS BY NIYI OSUNDARE

■ In some poems, such as this one, there is no doubt about the poet's attitude, because it is obvious from the start. We are shown what is happening in the society and how people react to it. They ignore the suffering of others and think only of themselves. The poet's feelings are revealed by:
  • the language used
  • how the situation is described.

They picked Akanni up one morning
Beat him soft like clay
And stuffed him down the belly
Of a waiting jeep.
     What business of mine is it
     So long they don't take the yam
     From my savouring mouth?

They came one night
Booted the whole house awake
And dragged Danladi out,
Then off to a lengthy absence.
     What business of mine is it
     So long they don't take the yam
     From my savouring mouth?

Chinwe went to work one day
Only to find her job was gone:
No query, no warning, no probe –
Just one neat sack for a stainless record.
     What business of mine is it
     So long they don't take the yam
     From my savouring mouth?

The simile makes Akanni appear powerless and beaten to a pulp.

'stuffed' suggests inhuman treatment.

We hear exactly what the man says who does not want to be involved.

He is presented as insensitive and concerned only with the delights of eating: a contrast and link with the jeep that has others in its belly. The man's lack of concern is made to seem morally unacceptable.

■ Ironically, the fact that the speaker has tried not to get involved does not save him. His turn comes too:

He was more interested In his yams than in his neighbours' problems.

His eating stops. He is metaphorically frozen with fear.

He was silent when others were taken, so it is fitting there is silence when they come for him: silence represents the lack of opposition.

And then one evening
As I sat down to eat my yam
A knock on the door froze my hungry hand.
The jeep was waiting on my bewildered lawn
Waiting, waiting in its usual silence.

- In this poem, the fact that the man does nothing to help does not save him. Despite his attempts to avoid it, he still faces suffering at the end. Because the speaker seems to care little for his neighbours, there is a sad appropriateness when the jeep finally arrives for him, and the poet leads us to a clear message: inaction leads to the suffering of all.

- When writing about the message, of course, it is vital to explain exactly what you mean and to support your comments with close reference to the poem. In this example, a candidate was asked:

  - to explain the poet's attitude to what happens in the poem
  - what the reader can learn from the poem.

From the opening stanza, the poem is based on a contrast. We have four lines of persecution, then three lines in which the speaker dissociates himself from what is happening around him.

The suffering is personalised by the use of names (Akanni, Danladi and Chinwe), and intensified by the use of detail. Akanni, for instance, is beaten 'soft like clay', whilst, when they come for Danladi, they 'booted the whole house awake'. Violence is foremost in both incidents. At the same time, there is a frightening sense of mystery: Danladi goes for 'a lengthy absence' and Chinwe's job is taken for no clear reason.

Such happenings grab our attention and sympathy; yet the speaker seems callous, and continues to eat yams, look after himself and ignore the injustice around him. His 'savouring mouth' should be speaking out, not eating comfortably and well. The way he is presented makes him seem almost as bad as the jeep which 'eats' those who are being persecuted.

However, the poet shows us that hoping to avoid trouble does not lead to escape from oppression.

The 'knock on the door' at the end is terrifying and even stops the speaker eating. The frozen moment is accompanied by silence, which is perhaps fitting in this case, because this is where our silence leads: to the jeep for us all. The final stanza is not broken into two parts, because there is no longer any difference between the speaker and the victims – his time has come.

GOOD POINTS:

- The poet's attitude is revealed through the approaches used:
  1. the personalisation of those suffering, and the violence and mystery of the aggressors
  2. the contrast between the way the speaker behaves and the injustice he ignores
  3. the way in which the situations are presented so we cannot avoid being critical of the speaker.
- The moral of the poem is made clear.

⚡ A* EXTRA

- One key to a top grade is to focus on the poet's message by analysing three elements:
  - What is said?
  - How is it presented?
  - Why is it presented in that way?
- Top candidates respond evaluatively to the language: *The 'knock...' is terrifying,* and *which is perhaps fitting.* Comments which show you have a personal response to the verse will gain extra marks.

◎ Comparing *Vultures* and *Not my Business*

■ Comparison will be required, whichever question you choose to answer in the examination. It is always useful, therefore, to revise poems in pairs. In the examination, the questions may not allow you to use a particular pair you have prepared, but the fact that you have practised using comparative techniques will be of enormous benefit.

In the case of *Vultures* and *Not my Business,* there are various elements to compare and contrast. For example:

	Vultures	Not my Business
Similarities		
evil	The grim behaviour of the birds and the Commandant: 'fumes of / human roast clinging / rebelliously to his hairy / nostrils'	The violence and unfairness visited on the people: 'Just one neat sack for a stainless record'
feeding	The birds and the Commandant's child eat well: 'chocolate / for his tender offspring'	The pleasure of eating yams allows the speaker to ignore what is happening: 'So long they don't take the yam / From my savouring mouth'
Differences		
love	Between the birds, and in the Commandant's family: 'a tiny glow-worm / tenderness'	There is no love. The jeep and its occupants seem to show no mercy and are not personalised: 'The jeep was waiting'
nature/mankind link	Nature and mankind seen as similar in love and cruelty: 'in… that kindred love is / lodged the perpetuity / of evil'	No normal, natural feeling for others: 'Booted the whole house awake'
time and place	Evil in mankind pictured in Second World War, in concentration camp: Belsen	Apparently an African setting, and it could be contemporary
message	Love and evil co-exist in living creatures	If men do not support each other, their situation is hopeless, and there will be no end to the suffering

CHECK YOURSELF QUESTION

Q • What happens in this poem?

• What is the poet's attitude to it?

• What message can we take from the poem and in what way is it different from the message in *Not my Business*?

Blessing

The skin cracks like a pod.
There never is enough water.

Imagine the drip of it,
the small splash, echo
in a tin mug,
the voice of a kindly god.

Sometimes, the sudden rush
of fortune. The municipal pipe bursts,
silver crashes to the ground
and the flow has found
a roar of tongues. From the huts,
a congregation: every man woman
child for streets around
butts in, with pots,
brass, copper, aluminium,
plastic buckets,
frantic hands,
and naked children
screaming in the liquid sun,
their highlights polished to perfection,
flashing light,
as the blessing sings
over their small bones.

Imtiaz Dharker

Answer is on pages 150–151.

Structure

You could be asked about the structure of two poems.

This would mean analysing:

- how each poem is presented on the page: its layout (stanzas, line length and so on)
- how each poem is organised: how it opens, develops and concludes. You might have to show how the structure is appropriate for the poet's message, and explain how the stucture affects the reader's understanding.

⊚ How the poem is presented

- In some cases, the visual impression created by a poem is striking. For example, *from Unrelated Incidents* by Tom Leonard replicates a television autocue, as if the poet is reading from it: an ironic activity for someone who would not be allowed to read the news on television (see page 32).

- The different line lengths and indentations which are a feature of Lawrence Ferlinghetti's *Two Scavengers in a Truck, Two Beautiful People in a Mercedes* suggest the movement in the travellers' lives and a shifting modern existence, which has no uniformity. Life flows on but is shredded:

enjambements (lack of punctuation at end of lines) so the sentence runs on, like life itself

> At the stoplight waiting for the light
> nine a.m. downtown San Francisco
> a bright yellow garbage truck
> with two garbagemen in red plastic blazers
> standing on the back stoop
> one on each side hanging on
> and looking down into
> an elegant open Mercedes
> with an elegant couple in it

The poem gives the impression of someone speaking, with their pauses indicated by the breaks in lines and continuity. In places, the enjambements and indentations give emphasis to what follows:

'and looking down into
an elegant open Mercedes
with an elegant couple in it'.

The reader drops to the next line, as does the gaze of the garbagemen, noticing first the car, then, standing out from it, the 'elegant couple'.

Other effects are evident too. For instance, the garbage truck is near the start of a line, whereas the Mercedes is at the end - as if it is ahead of the truck, as the couple are socially ahead of the garbagemen.

GOOD POINTS:

Presentational features are explained, rather than just identified –
- 'The reader drops to the next line…'
- 'as if it is ahead of the truck, as the couple are ahead…'

How the poem is organised

1. GENERAL STRUCTURE

■ Our reaction to a poem is influenced not only by the layout but also by how the poet has chosen to organise it: how the poet deals with the ideas and how the content is ordered.

■ Ferlinghetti describes a moment when people from two very different cultures are briefly together in the traffic. In some ways, we seem to be looking at a picture, with:

> both scavengers gazing down
> as from a great distance
> at the cool couple
> as if they were watching some odorless TV ad...

The poem opens with mention of the stoplight, and ends with a similar reference. There has been no movement.

■ In contrast, *Night of the Scorpion* by Nissim Ezekiel is a narrative, which begins with a personal pronoun and tells a personal story:

> I remember the night my mother
> was stung by a scorpion.

The poem is an account, rather than a description, although descriptive elements are apparent (for example, how the peasants behave and what the atmosphere is like). The poem moves, to some extent chronologically, through what happens to Ezekiel's mother during twenty hours. It tells:
* what the scorpion did
* how the neighbours react
* how the incident is given a religious significance
  (May the poison purify your flesh)
* of father's efforts to cure her
* what happens at the end.

■ Yet both poems move to a clear conclusion. In the case of *Two Scavengers in a Truck*, there is an ironic comment:

> as if anything at all were possible
> between them

This is ironic because the layout of these lines seems to be saying something else. In reality, the two sets of people are separated by a 'gulf' in lifestyles that is made apparent by the way 'between them' is set apart so that it does not fit with the line above.

Also there is the uneasiness of the shifting nature of the lines on the page

> across that small gulf
> in the high seas
> of this democracy.

The reader is made aware of how the lines mirror the sea's movement, as if the people have only been washed together for the moment, by the tide of existence.

■ *Night of the Scorpion*, meanwhile, is in solid blocks of text and illustrates the strength of the woman, her trust in God and love for her family. Despite all her suffering, we hear her speak for the first time right at the end:

> My mother only said
> Thank God the scorpion picked on me
> and spared my children.

This ending gives the incident a sense of being nothing out of the ordinary, yet it also emphasises the woman's – and the culture's – priorities. The mother's words are contained in their own short stanza to emphasise their significance.

2. STRUCTURAL DEVICES

■ The poems in the Anthology use a variety of structural devices. For example:

- *Limbo* has a repeated refrain, which constantly reminds us of the dance and the situation of the slaves:

> limbo
> limbo like me

   (while on the page, its shape mimics the movements of the dancers as they go in and out and up and down).

- *Nothing's Changed* shows, through its pattern, how nothing changes: stanzas 1 and 7 are about the poet's situation and mood; stanzas 2 and 3, like 5 and 6, show the contrasts; and the poem hinges on the two lines of stanza 4, which sum up the society:

> No sign says it is:
> but we know where we belong.

- *Not my Business* employs stanzas which break into two parts: what is happening to others, then how the speaker is reacting, his disregard for the others emphasised as he seems to chant a regular mantra, as if to shut out all knowledge of what is happening to them:

> What business of mine is it
> So long they don't take the yam
> From my savouring mouth?

- *Half-Caste* relies heavily on repetition to challenge the listener/reader's preconceptions:

> Explain yuself
> wha yu mean.

- *Vultures* has a stanza about the birds, followed by a stanza generalising about what this shows of life; and this is mirrored by a stanza about the Commandant, followed by another which again generalises, linking clearly the birds and the man.

⚡ **A* EXTRA**

▸ For each of the poems you have studied, try to decide:
  • how it is set out on the page
  • how the information is organised
  • how refrains, repetition or stanzas have been used.
▸ In each case, consider the effect upon the reader: the structure will have been chosen to support or emphasise the poet's message.

CHECK YOURSELF QUESTION

Q • How is this poem structured?

• Why has it been structured in this way?

• How successful is this structure?

• Compare the structure with that of another poem you have studied.

What Were They Like?

1) Did the people of Viet Nam
   use lanterns of stone?
2) Did they hold ceremonies
   to reverence the opening of buds?
3) Were they inclined to quiet laughter?
4) Did they use bone and ivory,
   jade and silver, for ornament?
5) Had they an epic poem?
6) Did they distinguish between speech and singing?

1) Sir, their light hearts turned to stone.
   It is not remembered whether in gardens
   stone lanterns illumined pleasant ways.
2) Perhaps they gathered once to delight in blossom,
   but after the children were killed
   there were no more buds.
3) Sir, laughter is bitter to the burned mouth.
4) A dream ago, perhaps. Ornament is for joy.
   All the bones were charred.
5) It is not remembered. Remember,
   most were peasants; their life
   was in rice and bamboo.
   When peaceful clouds were reflected in the paddies
   and the water buffalo stepped surely along terraces,
   maybe fathers told their sons old tales.
   When bombs smashed those mirrors
   There was time only to scream.
6) There is an echo yet
   of their speech which was like a song.
   It was reported that their singing resembled
   the flight of moths in moonlight.
   Who can say? It is silent now.

                                   Denise Levertov

Answer is on
page 151.

Language

Whatever question you decide to answer, you will need to write about the language in the poems. You need to know how the poets have used:
- poetic techniques
- general language features: vocabulary, sentences and punctuation.

You will also need to explain what effect the language in different poems has on the reader.

◎ Poetic techniques

- Most poems employ a range of poetic techniques.

- For example, poems may contain similes, comparisons using 'like' or 'as':

  The peasants came like swarms of flies
  — *Night of the Scorpion* by Nissim Ezekiel

The comparison of the peasants to flies makes them seem not altogether pleasant, and rather mindless.

  trees / Falling heavy as whales

  — *Hurricane Hits England* by Grace Nichols

Comparing the trees to whales makes the reader understand that the winds are strong enough to blow over even trees that are as substantial as whales, linking to the Caribbean background.

- This extract from *Limbo* by Kamau Braithwaite contains a range of other techniques:

And limbo stick is the silence in front of me
limbo

limbo
limbo like me
limbo
limbo like me

long dark night is the silence in front of me
limbo
limbo like me

stick hit sound
and the ship like it ready

stick hit sound
and the dark still steady

limbo
limbo like me

long dark deck and the water surrounding me
long dark deck and the silence is over me

rhythm – which becomes most apparent when poetry is read aloud: rhythm of the song and dance here

enjambement – lines not ended with punctuation because dance is on-going and slaves' suffering has no end
repetition – to create mesmeric effect of dance
assonance – repeated vowel sound ('stick', 'hit', 'ship'): sounds of the ship

rhyme – repetition of the word endings emphasises the repetitive nature of life on the ship

alliteration – where words which are close together begin with the same letter: the repeated 'd's suggest both footsteps in the dance and the blows of punishment

> *limbo*
> *limbo like me*
>
> stick is the whip
> and the dark deck is slavery
>
> stick is the whip
> and the dark deck is slavery
>
> *limbo*
> *limbo like me*
>
> drum stick knock
> and the darkness is over me…

metaphor – where something is not literally true: the pain is represented as being part of the dance

symbol – where something represents something else: here, the stick symbolises the repression of the slaves

onomatopoeia – where sounds are captured in words, so that we can hear the sound as we read the text

■ It is never enough just to identify poetic techniques. The examiner is looking for an explanation of why they have been used and the effect they are creating.

This is how techniques used in *Limbo* might be analysed:

In *Limbo*, Braithwaite sets out to show the situation and suffering of the slaves, as they are transported to America. Underpinning the whole poem is the rhyme and the rhythm of the dance; the slaves, perhaps, dance and chant to remember their homeland; or maybe they are just dancing to the white man's tune. There is the repeated refrain:

'*limbo*
limbo like me'

as if the dance – and, perhaps, their suffering – simply goes on and on. This is further suggested by the repetition in the poem, and by the general lack of punctuation: we feel the horror is unremitting, until the very end of the poem, with its one full-stop.

The poem also relies on metaphor and symbol. The 'stick' represents the way in which the slaves are repressed and, no doubt, beaten. The stick is their master. The 'dark deck' stands for their metaphorical slavery – it suggests a deck packed with the slaves, or even a deck stained with blood. The darkness also implies that light and joy have gone from their lives. The alliteration of 'd's makes it sound dismal and depressing.

As well as the rhythm and the refrain, the reader is also presented with other sounds from the ship. There is the onomatopoeia as the stick provides the beat:

'drum stick knock'.

These three sounds do not stand alone, though. We also hear the swish of a beating:

'stick is the whip'.

The hardness of 'stick' – a word repeated throughout the poem, for emphasis – is transferred, using assonance, to the whisking of 'whip'…

GOOD POINTS:

- The use of poetic techniques is linked to the poet's overall purpose.
- There is explanation of how the techniques have been used, rather than just simple identification.
- A personal interpretation is offered, with the candidate giving an overview then showing how she interprets the poem's features.

General language features

- Just as, in Paper 1, you examine the language of texts, so, in Paper 2, you also need to judge the effect of particular vocabulary, punctuation and sentences in poems. These language features will have been chosen by the poet to create meaning, develop ideas or add significance.

- In the following poem, the annotations show
  - language features (green)
  - significant details and feelings (blue)
  - how the poem builds/how the reactions are structured (orange)

The poem deals with how coming to terms with ourselves brings peace, perhaps more even than any relationship.

Love After Love

The time will come — joy is stressed from the start
When, with elation, — commas serve to highlight the emotion
You will greet yourself arriving
At your own door, in your own mirror, — 'own' repeated to emphasise 'yourself' is core of poem
And each will smile at the other's welcome,

And say sit here. Eat. — second 'And' builds effect to simple 'Eat': simple pleasure then indicated by one-word sentence
You will love again the stranger who was your self.
Give wine. Give bread. Give back your heart — wine and bread give religious significance
To itself, to the stranger who has loved you — repetition of 'heart' appropriate in this love poem

All your life, whom you ignored
For another, who knows you by heart. — list of what must be done to love again
Take down the love-letters from the bookshelf — no punctuation, suggesting this activity runs straight into the next

The photographs, the desperate notes,
Peel your own images from the mirror. — idea of celebrating, enjoying life again, in short sentences: simple advice following removal of complexity of old life, represented by previous more complex sentences
Sit. Feast on your life.

imperatives

- Clearly, Derek Walcott is using a range of linguistic techniques and they do not just support his message; they actually create the meanings we understand as readers.

This is an analysis of his poem:

Walcott is writing a poem intended to give the reader confidence that, as life goes on, each of us will be happy with our own self and what we really are. From the beginning, he focuses on happiness ('elation', 'smiling'), stresses that we are in our 'own' environment and can enjoy the experience.

It is as if we are returning to simple pleasures. 'Eat' is a one-word sentence, but stresses the fact that we can feed ourselves – we do not need others. In fact, there is a kind of religious communion, with the mention of: 'Give wine. Give bread'. This notion is repeated later ('Feast on your life'). It is as if we have enough memories and knowledge to sustain us as long as we live. The sentences the poet uses help to support his message. In the last two stanzas, there are relatively complex sentences, as the old life is dismantled, and one line lacks the necessary punctuation at the end, as if to suggest it should be carried out quickly and we should move rapidly to the next action:

'Take down the love-letters from the bookshelf'.

The list of which this is a part, along with:

'The photographs, the desperate notes...'

forms a clutter of activities which contrast with the simplicity of the ending:

'Sit. Feast on your life.'

This is all showing that everything will be easier and simpler when we have come to terms with what we really are.

Throughout, though, there are imperative verbs telling the reader exactly what is required: 'Eat... Give... Take down... Peel... Sit... Feast...' They help the poet persuade and advise the reader, and show Walcott's confidence and conviction.

GOOD POINTS:

- Language features are analysed to show how they help the poet achieve his purpose.
- There are precise references to the poem.
- Comments on vocabulary, sentence forms and punctuation have all been integrated into this answer.

A* EXTRA

▸ Linking message with method is a high order skill that will be rewarded with high marks.

◎ Comparing language use

- Language is obviously used differently in different poems. Part of the comparison you carry out in the exam should deal with how language has been used in the poems about which you choose to write. This will be a relevant part of your response, no matter how the question is phrased.

Look at how it is used in these two extracts:

This room is breaking out of itself, cracking through its own walls	vocabulary of hatching
	enjambements
in search of space, light, empty air.	list
	vocabulary of upward movement
The bed is lifting out of its nightmares. From dark corners, chairs are rising up to crash through clouds.	contrast: dark, shift to open sky
This Room by Imtiaz Dharker	onomatopoeia and alliteration

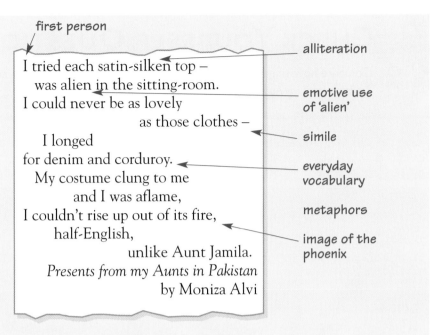

first person

alliteration

emotive use of 'alien'

simile

everyday vocabulary

metaphors

image of the phoenix

> I tried each satin-silken top –
>   was alien in the sitting-room.
> I could never be as lovely
>   as those clothes –
>   I longed
> for denim and corduroy.
>   My costume clung to me
>   and I was aflame,
> I couldn't rise up out of its fire,
>   half-English,
>   unlike Aunt Jamila.
> *Presents from my Aunts in Pakistan*
>   by Moniza Alvi

■ An analysis of the use of language in these poems needs to include these points, and must also compare the poems, wherever that is appropriate.

Here is one student's analysis of language use...

✔

Whereas Dharker's poem is positive, with vivid images of improvement, Alvi seems trapped. In 'This Room', chairs 'are rising', but Alvi 'couldn't rise up': the house, symbolising Dharker's life, is being re-born, but Alvi is not like a phoenix, and it seems that although her clothes are colourful, she is just being metaphorically consumed by her existence: 'I was aflame'.

After the initial metaphors of hatching ('breaking out' and 'cracking'), Dharker introduces a list which offers openness: 'space, light, / empty air'. Then, we have 'lifting' and onomatopoeia and the use of 'c's, producing a climax with the alliteration of 'crash through clouds'.

Alvi, though, is describing a life which lacks that rush of optimism. Using alliteration, she contrasts the softness of the Pakistani clothes ('satin-silken') with the more basic British clothes she really desires: 'denim and corduroy'. The words themselves sound modern and western. The presents are more exotic but she explains in a simile she 'could never be as lovely as those clothes'. Between two cultures, she feels out of place and seems out of hope...

GOOD POINTS:

- Each text is being handled in detail.
- Comparisons are being made.
- The analysis includes both poetic techniques and general language features.

There are many more points still to cover.

CHECK YOURSELF QUESTION

Q Compare how language has been used in the endings of *This Room* and *Presents from my Aunts in Pakistan.*

This Room

Pots and pans bang together
In celebration, clang
Past the crowd of garlic, onions, spices,
Fly by the ceiling fan.
No one is looking for the door.

In all this excitement
I'm wondering where
I've left my feet, and why

My hands are outside, clapping.

Presents from my Aunts in Pakistan

Sometimes I saw Lahore –
        my aunts in shaded rooms,
screened from male visitors,
    sorting presents,
        wrapping them in tissue.

Or there were beggars, sweeper-girls
    and I was there –
        of no fixed nationality,
staring through fretwork
        at the Shalimar Gardens.

Answer is on page 152.

Selecting and using textual references

The questions on Paper 2 will expect you to compare two poems. Sessions 1–4 of this Unit have already dealt with different aspects that you will probably need to compare.

This session concentrates on:
- the technique you will need to adopt for answering the question in the exam
- how to make clear comparisons.

◎ Examination technique

■ Ideally, a response should have:
  - a brief introduction, related to the title which has been set
  - detailed comparison of the poems
  - a brief conclusion, perhaps considering the success of the poems, in terms of what the question has asked you to focus on.

Consider this exam question:

> Compare *Nothing's Changed* with another poem from a different culture or tradition. Show how the people in the poems react to their surroundings.

The following annotations show some approaches to *Nothing's Changed* and *Island Man* which would help you to respond to this question. They show:
- language features (green)
- significant details and feelings (blue)
- how the poem builds/how the reactions are structured (orange).

Nothing's Changed by Tatamkhulu Afrika

Small round hard stones click	monosyllables and onomatopoeia: harsh-sounding
under my heels,	opening description of District Six
seeding grasses thrust	
bearded seeds	run-down surroundings
into trouser cuffs, cans,	
trodden on, crunch	onomatopoeia: crushing sounds
in tall, purple-flowering,	details stretch through the stanza, like the district stretches out
amiable weeds.	
District Six.	two-word sentence: impact
No board says it is:	
but my feet know,	stanza deals with personal reaction
and my hands,	surroundings affect every part of him
and the skin about my bones,	
and the soft labouring of my lungs,	list and repeated 'and' building to climax
and the hot, white, inwards turning	enjambement and adjectives: surging emotion
anger of my eyes.	emotional upset builds to climax

Poem	Annotation
Brash with glass,	sounds glaring, unavoidable
name flaring like a flag,	simile and alliteration: seems outstanding and symbolic
it squats	sounds like an intruder or an ugly toad
in the grass and weeds,	dislike of the restaurant
incipient Port Jackson trees:	stanza focuses on identifiable target
new, up-market, haute cuisine,	
guard at the gatepost,	rough, threatening 'g's
whites only inn.	bitterness and ambiguity
	break from next two lines lends them weight
No sign says it is:	central two lines in poem sum up core of emotional upset
but we know where we belong.	sarcasm
I press my nose	
to the clear panes, know,	'know' ('nose') repeated, showing certainty
before I see them, there will be	
crushed ice white glass,	stanza describes the inn
linen falls,	can appreciate the signs of luxury
the single rose.	elegant imagery
Down the road,	'down' contrast to 'up-market'
working man's café sells	
bunny chows.	'basic' facilities for blacks
Take it with you, eat	
it at a plastic table's top,	clear contrast for effect
wipe your fingers on your jeans,	list sounds like an everyday routine
spit a little on the floor:	
it's in the bone.	cynical comment
I back from the glass,	ending personal and threatens action
boy again,	
leaving small mean O	feels like an under-privileged child
of small, mean mouth.	repeated phrasing for emphasis
Hands burn	
for a stone, a bomb,	violent emotions: use of 'b's and
to shiver down the glass.	a kind of nightmare onomatopoeia in 'shiver'
Nothing's changed.	explanation of anger: repetition 'frames' poem and shows nothing has changed

'regular' 8-line stanzas give impression poet has considered and structured his ideas

Island Man by Grace Nichols

(for a Caribbean island man in London who still wakes up to the sound of the sea)

Morning	one-word opening sets scene
and island man wakes up	opens with scenes of Caribbean
to the sound of blue surf	initially, he seems at home
in his head	
the steady breaking and wombing	onomatopoeia adds sounds to colour of home
wild seabirds	individual details for impact atmosphere of the islands
and fishermen pushing out to sea	lively vocabulary of movement
the sun surfacing defiantly	lack of punctuation reveals movement/life
from the east	dreaming of/remembering the island
of his small emerald island	adjective makes setting vivid
he always comes back groggily groggily	repetition: seems dazed and space on line captures the break, then grogginess, in his return to reality
Comes back to sands	repeated 'comes back' as if insistent
of a grey metallic soar	urban metaphor unpleasant city
to surge of wheels	sounds: tyres on wet road layout: wheels rolling forward
to dull North Circular roar	contrasting noises: onomatopoeia
	two worlds collide: contrasting description
muffling, muffling	repetition: noises relatively faint
his crumpled pillow waves	metaphor: other world in his dreams
island man heaves himself	drags himself out of bed, into London life
	'heaves' shows effort required
Another London day	unspectacular – just 'another' separation of line emphasises its reality and breaks it away from his more pleasant dream

Opening paragraph

In 'Nothing's Changed', we are presented with a picture of South Africa after the end of apartheid. The poet is suggesting that life has not improved, and has produced a protest poem which shows the inequalities and unfairness in that country. The situation in 'Island Man' is different, because Grace Nichols reveals how a Caribbean island man still thinks of his home, but has to get up and cope with existence in the country to which he has moved. He may not be happy, but has chosen this way of living.

poem summarised briefly

relates to title: the poet's message

clear comparison made

poem summarised briefly

relates to title: how man reacts

GOOD POINTS:

- The candidate focuses on the title.
- Poems are summarised quickly, because their general content is not the focus for the response.
- From the start, the candidate compares the poems.

Concluding paragraph

Tatamkhulu Afrika, therefore, considers violence as the only answer. The final stanza leaves the reader with the image of a bomb smashing the glass which is symbolically keeping apart the two communities, and the last line effectively returns us to the start, because, as we learnt in the title, 'Nothing's changed'. 'Island Man', however, seems resigned to his life, accepts the traffic noise because he must and leaves behind his dreams for 'Another London day'. The contrast between his life as it was and his life as it is, though, has been made very clear, and there does not appear to be the energy in him there once was.

moves us to a conclusion

relates to title

implies success

over-view of the poem's message and mention of technique

clear comparison

over-view of poem's perspective

deals with poem's success

GOOD POINTS:

- The candidate weaves in some evaluation of the poems' success.
- The candidate still has the title clearly in mind.
- This has continued to be a comparative response.

⚡ A* EXTRA

▸ If your conclusion deals with similar issues to your introduction, but your ideas have moved on because of what you have said in the body of your response, an examiner will recognise that you are working at a high level.

◎ Making clear comparisons

■ As well as mentioning points of comparison in the opening and concluding paragraphs, you need to compare clearly in the body of your answer. There are different ways of handling this.

For example, you might choose:

METHOD 1
● write in detail about one poem

then

● write about the second poem, referring back to the first to make your comparisons

or:

METHOD 2
● write about aspects of the two poems together, fully integrating the ideas and features.

METHOD 1

If you had written about *Nothing's Changed* first, the next section on *Island Man* might well be punctuated by the following sorts of statements:

> When we examine 'Island Man', we see that his situation is similar in that he, too, can imagine a better life. In his case, though, it is a beautiful life he has known already:
> 'the sound of blue surf...
> and fishermen pushing out to sea...'
>
> Whereas Africa can see no hope for black people in South Africa and feels like turning to violence, Grace Nichols shows us Island Man apparently accepting his situation:
> 'he always comes back...'
>
> The sense of anger in Africa's language does not occur in Nichols' poem. Instead, we hear the wash of the waves ('breaking and wombing'), and can feel the wonder of life in the Caribbean on a 'small emerald island', which sounds like a jewel, contrasting with the barren picture of District Six...
>
> Even the structure of the poem is very different from 'Nothing's Changed'. Africa's poem is built of almost regular eight line stanzas but 'Island Man' is irregular and freer, perhaps like the man's spirit... and instead of ending with hate and violence, it moves to the reality of 'Another London day'. The phrase is all alone and hangs, unavoidable, at the end, like the spectre of life in Britain's capital that awaits the man every morning...

Examining the two poems together is a more difficult skill, especially if you have not revised the two poems as a pair. It is likely to mean dealing with an attitude, then comparing it with the second; directly comparing elements of language; setting the structures side by side, and so on.

This is an extract from the middle section of such a response:

> Island Man comes from a culture which seems close to nature, calm and relaxed:
>
> > 'wakes up
> > to the sound of blue surf'.
>
> This romantic image of the sea, supported by the soft onomatopoeia of 'breaking and wombing', makes the memory a treasure. It is very different from the harsh realities of life in South Africa. The verbs used by the poet at the start of that poem sound sharp, and make the environment appear desolate, whilst the mood is one of despondency or aggression: 'click', 'thrust', 'trodden on', 'crunch'.
>
> In the second stanza, Africa uses a list and repetition of 'and' to build to what seems a climax of rage at the unfairness in the country:
>
> > 'and the hot, white, inwards turning
> > anger of my eyes.'
>
> The whiteness suggests his emotions have become molten; whilst Nichols captures a much more relaxed scene by using 'blue surf' and 'small emerald island'. Here, we have warmth, not heat, and the use of 'emerald' shows the island is a jewel to be treasured...

⚡ A* EXTRA

▶ The weaving together and comparison of different elements of two poems is a skill recognised and rewarded by examiners with a high mark.

Island Man's culture identified: setting and atmosphere

clear comparison made

grim picture of life in South Africa contrasted with Island Man's soft romanticism

emotion detailed, which grows from the circumstances already described

further comparison: in attitude: warm colours, contrasted with the white heat

GOOD POINTS:

- Relevant points from the two poems are juxtaposed – set side by side – and compared.
- The response remains detailed, with precise quotations and explanations.

CHECK YOURSELF QUESTION

Q Show how *Half-Caste* and one other poem from a different culture present the feelings of people who do not feel part of 'mainstream' society.

Write about:
• the problems the people have
• their feelings
• how successfully their feelings are shown.

(The sample answer compares this poem with *from Search for My Tongue* so you might find it useful to tackle this comparison too.)

Half-Caste

Excuse me
standing on one leg
I'm half-caste

Explain yuself
wha yu mean
when yu say half-caste
yu mean when picasso
mix red an green
is a half-caste canvas/
explain yuself
wha yu mean
when yu say half-caste
yu mean when light an shadow
mix in de sky
is a half-caste weather/
well in dat case
england weather
nearly always half-caste
in fact some o dem cloud
half-caste till dem overcast
so spiteful dem dont want de sun pass
ah rass/
explain yuself
wha yu mean
when yu say half-caste
yu mean tchaikovsky
sit down at dah piano
an mix a black key
wid a white key
is a half-caste symphony/

Explain yuself
wha yu mean
Ah listening to yu wid de keen
half of mih ear
Ah lookin at yu wid de keen
half of mih eye
and when I'm introduced to yu
I'm sure you'll understand
why I offer yu half-a-hand
an when I sleep at night
I close half-a-eye
consequently when I dream
I dream half-a-dream
an when moon begin to glow
I half-caste human being
cast half-a-shadow
but yu must come back tomorrow
wid de whole of yu eye
an de whole of yu ear
and de whole of yu mind

an I will tell yu
de other half
of my story

John Agard

Answer is on page 152.

WRITING SKILLS

Section B of both English papers requires you to produce a Writing response in 45 minutes. This will mean writing 1–2 sides. Paper 1 requires you to write to argue, persuade and advise, and Paper 2 requires you to inform, explain and describe. These different styles of writing are dealt with in depth in *Types of Writing*, pages 82–119.

Both papers will also be testing the general quality of your Writing, and those skills will be dealt with in this section: the way you generate and use ideas, your structure and paragraphing, the variety of your sentences and vocabulary, and the accuracy of your punctuation and spelling.

◉ Ideas

■ You will be assessed on your ability to:

I. *Communicate clearly and imaginatively, using and adapting forms for different readers and purposes.*

This means you must know about how to write in different genres (see *Types of Writing*, pages 82–119), but you must also be able to produce ideas which are matched to the task and imaginative enough to engage and sustain the reader's interest.

- See Session 1

◉ Structure and paragraphing

■ You will be assessed on your ability to:

2. *Organise ideas into paragraphs and whole texts using a variety of structural features.*

It is not enough to have a number of ideas. The way you structure them within the response and your ability to write paragraphs of appropriate and effective lengths will also be significant features when marks are awarded.

- See Session 2

◎ Sentences

■ You will be assessed on your ability to:

3. *Organise ideas into sentences, and use a range of sentence structures effectively.*

    The quality of your sentences is vital. They need to be varied and effective, which means using sentences of different length and complexity, and they must be appropriate for the purpose.

    - See Session 3

◎ Vocabulary

■ You will be assessed on your ability to:

4. *Organise ideas using a variety of linguistic features.*

    The quality of your vocabulary is often a clear indicator of your overall English ability. Your vocabulary must be suited to the form of writing, the purpose and audience. It must be varied to demonstrate your range and to avoid repetition and cliché. The best candidates' vocabulary is distinctive and carefully selected, so that the writing feels 'crafted'.

    - See Session 4

◎ Punctuation

■ You will be assessed on your ability to:

5. *Organise a range of sentences with accurate punctuation.*

    For a top grade, it is not enough to rely on full stops and capital letters. Producing 'a range of sentences' involves employing a range of punctuation correctly. This will include commas, apostrophes, exclamation marks and question marks, and might also include quotation marks, colons and semi-colons.

    - See Session 5

◎ Spelling

■ You will be assessed on your ability to:

6. *Use accurate spelling.*

    Incorrect spelling will affect how your writing is perceived and understood by the examiner. It will be penalised. You need to know how to spell words you use regularly and you should apply spelling rules whenever possible.

    - See Session 6

Generating ideas

On the exam paper, you will be advised to spend **five minutes planning** your response for Section B. The first stage in that process is **the generation of ideas** that you can use in your writing. The ideas you use should be:
- relevant
- developed (i.e. detailed)
- original wherever possible.

◎ Relevant ideas

STAGE 1

■ Your first priority is to identify the essential elements in the question title. It can be helpful to highlight the important words, to help you focus on them and identify the **purpose** and **audience**.

For example:

audience: will need clear but relatively basic advice, since they will be just starting the job

purpose: formal writing

> **1.** Write a **section for a school booklet** to be sent to **teachers applying for a job at your school.** Offer them **advice** on how to **cope with any problems** they might encounter.

purpose: to explain, not simply inform

purpose: to identify the problems and tell the new teachers exactly how they might cope with them

purpose: to focus on activities away from school/work

purpose: priority is to deal with term-time, not days during holidays

> **2.** Explain why you spend your free time in the way you do. Write about:
> - the way you spend evenings
> - what you do at weekends
> - why you find these activities interesting and worthwhile.

purpose: to give the reasons why you spend your time in these ways

■ Sometimes, especially on Paper 2, you will find questions like this with no stated audience: in that case, you are writing for the examiner. Your approach should still be relatively formal.

STAGE 2

■ Next assemble your ideas. Your initial thoughts are likely to be of a general nature, which can be developed and then structured (See Revision Session 2).

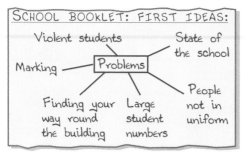

SCHOOL BOOKLET: FIRST IDEAS:

Violent students — State of the school

Marking — Problems

Finding your way round the building — Large student numbers — People not in uniform

■ You might choose to produce your ideas as a spider diagram, or begin to list them in the order you might deal with them in your actual response:

Free time
Evenings - homework, Tai Kwon Do, music, X Box
Weekends - town, football matches, cleaning (!), friends
Why - relaxation, fitness, self-improvement, a change from school and work

⊚ Developing ideas

- Although planning time is brief, if you develop the basic ideas you will benefit later: it will be easier to write the response itself, because you will know exactly what details to mention in each section.

- The ideas for the school booklet might be expanded in this way:

School booklet

Violent students:
Problem: aggressive attitude to teachers - regular fights during breaks - exclusions increasing
Advice: try listening and being understanding; don't be too strict but apply the rules

State of the school:
Problems: needs renovation - old desks - leaking roof - suffers vandalism
Advice: set an example by keeping your classroom tidy/get any graffiti removed that you see; set up after school litter patrols

People not in uniform:
Problems: trainers worn - Mrs Miller's crusade against nose studs! - regular detentions issued
Advice: give one chance, then issue detention; apply rules fairly; explain the reasons for uniforms

Finding your way round the building:
Problems: identical stairwells - all corridors the same - supply teachers starting to demand maps and compasses
Advice: ask sensible students for directions; use guides between lessons at first

Marking:
Problems: homework expected to be marked for next day - trouble getting books handed in - complex recording system
Advice: don't get behind or you'll never catch up - let students mark their own work sometimes

Large student numbers:
Problems: some sets over 30 - difficult to get to know all students in school - congestion in corridors - sometimes worse than M25
Advice: get to know your own form first - spot troublemakers - ask students to wear name badges

⚡ A* EXTRA

- Regular practice improves your ability to generate developed ideas quickly. Set yourself titles on any subjects of your choice – e.g. fashion, football or holidays – and assemble appropriate ideas.
- The titles should involve trying to argue, persuade, advise, inform, explain or describe (see *Types of Writing*, Revision Sessions 1-6). Try to spend no more than two or three minutes generating initial ideas for each title.

GOOD POINTS:

- The candidate has produced a range of relevant ideas, but has also supplemented them in places with originality – identified in red.
- There are several details in each section, which can be developed further when writing the response.

CHECK YOURSELF QUESTION

Q Collect the detailed ideas you would use to respond to the following title:

Write the text of a speech to be given to your year group, in which you attempt to persuade them to show more interest in what the school offers out of lesson time.

You might wish to mention:

• sports teams

• clubs and societies

• trips.

Answer is on page 153.

Structure and paragraphs

You will be awarded marks for your ability to structure your writing. The successful organisation of ideas requires:
- planning skills
- appropriate and creative use of paragraphs.

◎ Planning skills

■ Although you may have ideas on a given topic, it is not sufficient simply to write about them in any random order. An ideal response should have:

- an introductory paragraph which 'grabs the reader's attention'

- a logical development of ideas, divided into paragraphs of appropriate length through the central section

- a conclusion or ending, as a separate paragraph, which sticks in the mind of the examiner and relates clearly to what has gone before.

■ Your first task, therefore, is to place your ideas into the order in which you intend to deal with them and make those ideas as detailed as possible in the time available: you will be recommended to spend five minutes on planning in the exam.

■ In that time, you might produce something like this example. The response is broken into sections which, in most cases, will also represent the paragraphs you produce. In certain cases, you might wish to turn one of the sections into two or three shorter paragraphs.

> **Writing task**
> Describe the person you most admire in the world.

1. Uncle Frank: age, kind of person he is, how others see him, why he is my hero –
(1) Someone talking about him? or (2) anecdote?

2. How he found out about his illness. The effect it had: job/home.

3. Aunty Jane's situation. What she said. What they did. The outcome. Family involvement.

4. What he has been like since: with other people and on trips to the hospital.

5. Fund raising: his pain and his gains, reports in local paper, award from Queen

6. His future plans: – ending with hope,
(1) quotation from U.F. or (2) view of Aunty J.

GOOD POINTS:

- There are ideas to be expanded into an attention-grabbing introduction, development (in this case, partly chronological), and a conclusion which seems to grow logically from what has gone before.
- There is a 'core' idea in each section, then additional notes mapping out what might be included.
- The candidate has more than one idea of how to use the detail in the introduction and ending.

The introduction

- There are many ways in which you might begin any response – for example: with a description, a conversation, a moment of high drama, rhetorical questions and so on. It is always worth considering a number of approaches before deciding which one to choose. In the exam, there is no time to write them out, but do think hard about which might be most effective.

- Your first paragraph will, then, present your opening. It is likely to be about 60-70 words long and designed to grab the attention of the reader.

- In the case of 'Uncle Frank', there are two suggestions. Either would be suitable:

1. Someone talking about him

> Even our mayor admires my Uncle Frank, and hosted a dinner in his honour last year: 'What Frank has done is show just how much a person can achieve when they set their mind to it. He has overcome incredible disadvantages to work tirelessly for others, even though most people in his position might expect others to look after them. In the eyes of this town, he is a great man.'

relevant opening sentence – immediate sense of hero

quotation brings response – and Frank – to life

establishes Frank's qualities and situation

shows how highly Frank is regarded by all

GOOD POINTS:

- The first sentence brings the purpose into focus.
- Frank's heroic status is established quickly.

- The quotation makes Frank seem real and reveals that he does have admirable qualities.

2. Anecdote

> No one is like my Uncle Frank. I travelled with him on the bus to Outpatients, when the worst of the cancer still had him in its grip, and watched him give up his seat for a pregnant woman. He stood for nearly thirty minutes and never complained. As far as he is concerned, there is always someone worse off, always someone you can help. He is very special.

short, sharp, opening sentence

anecdote gives indication of his qualities

reveals his philosophy

ends with repeated judgment

GOOD POINTS:

- The simplicity of the first sentence is supported by the anecdote that follows.
- The anecdote puts Frank into a real setting and allows us almost to see him in action.

- The final sentence repeats the idea in the first, lending it emphasis, but by the end the reader is beginning to understand what makes him unique.

◎ The conclusion

■ However you decide to end a response, it should ideally be memorable and, whenever possible, link with the opening. It will generally be one paragraph, rounding off your piece of writing. It is likely to be about the same length as your opening.

In the case of 'Uncle Frank', whichever of the two suggestions in the plan were used, the final paragraph would refer back to the initial ideas:

1. Quotation from Uncle Frank

'I'm not great, like that mayor said,' Uncle Frank once told me, laughing. 'It was kind of him, but I'm just a stubborn man who does what he thinks is right. I've always lived like that, and I always will. I won't give in, but that's not special, it's just the way I am.' But he is special, of course. And that is why I admire him so much.

2. Aunty Jane's view

Aunty Jane knows him best, and she believes that if he ever needs urgent treatment he'll probably walk to the hospital, rather than call an ambulance. He won't want to inconvenience the ambulance driver! Or he'll go by bus, and give up his seat, as usual. He's a wonderful man. He's my hero.

GOOD POINTS:

- Both endings refer back to an opening paragraph.
- The spirit of Frank is captured, to conclude the response.
- The final sentences link directly to the title.

⚡ A* EXTRA

▸ Whether you are writing for Paper 1 or Paper 2, using quotations, anecdotes and examples *selectively* and *effectively* can make your writing more striking. These devices can bring openings to life and make endings memorable.

◎ Organising and linking paragraphs

■ How paragraphs are used gives the examiner a clear indication of the likely standard of the response:

E Grade	short tabloid paragraphs or over-lengthy ones
D Grade	mechanical paragraphs of the same length
C Grade	varied and linked paragraphs
B-A* Grades	paragraphs with clear relationships, which support and develop the meaning

■ Effective paragraphs are likely to have topic sentences to begin them and introduce what is to come. They present an idea which the paragraph then goes on to develop in more detail, as in the following examples:

The government has its priorities wrong... – to be followed by what is wrong or what should be the real priorities

There are seven steps to perfect happiness... – which will then be identified

You need to take care if your flight is to be without incident... – the paragraph will deal with safety requirements or the incidents which could occur.

■ Paragraphs can be linked in a variety of ways. Often you will decide to use a discourse marker, which is a word or phrase that can join paragraphs, or ideas within them. For example, you might use:

- chronological markers, like At first, Then and Later

- a sense of logical progression, using terms like Therefore, Consequently, As a result

- contrasting views, employing On the other hand, In contrast

- a simple ordering of ideas: Firstly, Secondly, Finally

- an extension of ideas: Because of this, What is more, In addition

and so on.

My holidays used to be boring: long mornings spent pretending to do the list of jobs my mother left me before she went to work; long afternoons in front of the television watching repeats and the dross of daytime television; and evenings gazing out of the window, wishing that something would happen – that anything would happen! It even seemed crazy to me at the time, but I wished school would start again, so that I could be back with friends. There is nothing more lonely than having to talk to a goldfish and trying to take a tortoise for walks round the garden.

Then, I met Garth, and my life was transformed. He smiled over the hedge and the sunshine beamed – he wasn't just a new neighbour, he was perfect.

Suddenly, I had a purpose. It was no longer a matter of filling the hours, it was all about trying to find enough time to get ready and to be with Garth and even to say goodnight. It was about looking my best and looking out for Garth and being half of a whole....

topic sentence introduces feelings about holidays

long opening paragraph with lists of boring activities captures the mood

chronological discourse marker and next topic sentence

short dramatic paragraph: contrasts to what went before and suggests life and change

discourse marker links to next paragraph and short topic sentence introduces more lively ideas

last paragraph of extract is built on a list which refers back to the topic sentence at the start, but contrasts with it: items are shorter, reflecting a more dynamic mood

GOOD POINTS:

- The paragraphs all have topic sentences, but they are very different: the length and construction of each is suitable for the content and mood.
- There are effective links: 'Then…', 'Suddenly…' These discourse markers link the new ideas with what has gone before, so the text extends logically and the reader can follow the developing stages.

CHECK YOURSELF QUESTION

Q   Improve the following response by:

- breaking it into paragraphs
- beginning each paragraph with one of the topic sentences provided
- within the paragraphs, choosing the appropriate discourse markers from those offered.

Title: Write a letter to a national newspaper to argue that the government should spend our taxes differently.

Response:

Dear Sir,

It seems incredible that so many millions of pounds are frittered away each year, whether we have a New Labour or Conservative Prime Minister. Surely, something could be done to use the money more wisely? We keep rushing off to fight in distant lands, and it does not seem to matter how much it will all cost. Funding can always be found. *Nevertheless/Yet/Although*, that cash could be spent in important and more constructive ways, either at home or abroad. Do the politicians ever consider alternative spending plans? It is, clearly, a way for many individuals to make a good living – especially the judges and barristers – but what do these eminent bodies achieve? Should we really be prepared to sit back and allow our tax revenues to be frittered away for ever? *In addition/ However/First*, millions more could be invested in our schools, colleges and universities. Instead of making students pay their tuition fees, we could avoid going to war for a year or two. That would probably provide enough cash to keep the students going for ten years or more. *On the contrary/Then/Come what may*, we could disband some of our forces and stop investing in more and more advanced armaments so that the hospitals and rail services could be moved into the twenty-first century. *What is more/In conclusion/Secondly*, we would have extra funding for aid work abroad. It all seems quite simple if you think logically. Every pound squandered is a pound that could have helped someone in need. It is time the people stood up for what is right and the politicians acted with more logic and humanity.

Yours faithfully…

Topic sentences

1. However, we need to act quickly.

2. I wonder how long the British people are going to accept the waste of public money by central government.

3. Similarly, there seem to be hundreds of committees and enquiries that have lives of their own, and budgets to match.

4. Just think about how much we spend on foreign wars and armaments.

5. There are alternative ways to use the money.

Answer is on page 154.

Sentences

Simple sentences

The types of sentences you use in your writing in Section B should be varied and appropriate. They must, obviously, make your meaning clear; but they must also have a tone which is suited to the needs of your purpose and audience.

You are likely to use simple, compound and complex sentences in your writing and you need to know how to use them effectively.

You may also want to include questions and exclamations although these need to be used sparingly and to produce a specific effect on the reader.

- Simple sentences are usually short and contain a subject and a verb.

  > He walked in.
  > The woman in the hat smiled at me.

- Simple sentences can be used in many ways. They can produce a feeling of simplicity but that does not mean they convey no emotion. For example, this moving incident from Ernest Hemingway's *A Farewell to Arms* is mostly made up of straightforward simple sentences:

  > 'Mrs Henry has had a haemorrhage... The doctor is with her.'
  >
  > 'Is it dangerous?'
  >
  > 'It is very dangerous.' The nurse went into the room and shut the door. I sat outside in the hall. Everything was gone inside of me. I did not think. I could not think. I knew she was going to die...'

  GOOD POINTS: ✔
  - The simplicity creates a sensation we can all understand ('I did not think. I could not think.')
  - The enormity of the moment is made greater, not lessened, by the short sentences.

- At other times, simple sentences can rush, one after the other, to provide excitement, as they do in this description:

  > He began to run. The man followed. His heart was racing. The man was catching him. He had no choice. He dived into the icy water.

- Or a short sentence can make a quick but powerful point:

  > The situation right across the country is one that leads many to despair. There are hospitals, struggling with under-funding and short of both staff and resources, that are endeavouring to keep our aging population on its feet and in its right mind whilst billions are being wasted on defence contracts and over-spending. It makes me angry.

  GOOD POINTS: ✔
  - The simple sentence at the end contrasts with what has gone before.
  - We might tend to agree with it because it seems such a straightforward statement and easy to understand.

- There are also sentences which do not conform to the usual rules. For instance, you might use a single word to create a particular effect:

  > We waited for more information from the governors. Nothing. What a waste of time!

- A very short sentence of this kind can be a powerful tool, but should not be used more than once or twice in any response, to maximise its effect.

A* EXTRA

▸ A carefully used simple sentence can have more power than another, more complex, one. Consider using one when you want to indicate firmly held belief or strong emotion or to focus on one single idea.

◎ Compound and complex sentences

- Simple sentences are effective when they are used sparingly and for the right reason. However, you will be expected to use compound and complex sentences as well.

- Compound sentences are created when simple sentences are linked together by a conjunction:

    The Prime Minister has not told the truth. He must resign.
    The Prime Minister has not told the truth, so he must resign.
    The Prime Minister has not told the truth and he must resign.

- Complex sentences involve a main clause and a subordinate clause or clauses, which would not make sense alone:

    Because the Prime Minister has not told the truth,
    he must resign.

    The Prime Minister must resign, if he has any sense
    of honour.

◎ Creating effects

- You need to read widely to become aware of the variety of effects that compound and complex sentences can produce.

- They may give a more restrained or considered feel to explanatory or argumentative writing:

    We cannot overlook the effect on the local wildlife and the
    general environment, which are bound to suffer. On the other
    hand, we know of the poverty of the local people and they
    must have a say in their own future.

or may provide more detail in descriptive writing:

    I see the old lady every summer, sitting at the bottom of
    the steps with her wise eyes and wide smile, and she seems
    unchanged by the years.

In the next section of the book, *Types of Writing*, you will find how these sorts of sentences can be used effectively in the different forms of writing.

This is an extract from a descriptive response which was awarded A*:

> At dawn, I woke to the lightening of the sky and the sound of distant crows in the woods behind the house. There was no traffic, just the animals in the fields and the lightest of breezes, rattling the window occasionally and shifting the curtains, which moved as if touched by faint ghosts. The house itself was otherwise silent, like a ship in a harbour. Then the children were about. The boards started to creak. There were loud voices down the hall. I stretched and began to think of pulling myself from the bed, settling my mind to face the day, whatever it might bring.

GOOD POINTS:

- The first three lengthy sentences create an impression of lethargy. Life seems unhurried, as if the narrator has the time to concentrate on exactly what is going on around her.
- The next three short sentences create more urgency as the house begins to wake up.
- The last long sentence mirrors the time taken to become fully awake.

■ This complex sentence builds to produce humour and a climax:

> Don't ask me how I managed to sit through The Matrix twice without understanding a word of it (though I do have a weakness for falling asleep during films with unlimited special-effects budgets), but I have now had a third go, this time on videotape with my 12-year-old hurriedly explaining one crucial bit to me while on screen something equally crucial is being hurriedly explained to Keanu Reeves, who to his credit looks as bewildered as I am, though of course Keanu doesn't have his wife asking why he can't just concentrate for goodness sake.
>
> Phil Hogan, writing in *The Observer Magazine*

GOOD POINTS:

• Even through such a long sentence, the writer keeps firm structural control.
• Hogan appears to be letting us into his thought processes.
• His confusion seems to be mirrored by the long and rambling sentence.
• The sentence builds to a climax, as his desperation seems to grow when his wife attacks his attitude.

Questions and exclamations

■ It is likely you will want to use one or more rhetorical questions. These do not expect an answer from the reader: rather, they are making a statement:

Do you know any school that has all the facilities it really needs?
• This implies: 'There are no schools that have all the facilities they need.'

Why do I spend my time designing clothes?
• This implies (depending on context): 'I waste my time designing clothes' or 'There are good reasons why I spend time designing clothes, and I am going to tell you what they are.'

■ You might also use exclamations. They demonstrate emotional reactions and aim to make the reader react the same way:

What a disgrace!
The results were stunning!

- Questions and exclamations should be used sparingly, so that they have an impact. If they are used too frequently, it will suggest your command of sentences is limited, rather than the opposite. They should also fit the form of your writing, the purpose and audience.

- The mark schemes for all the Section B responses expect examiners to reward their use. Nevertheless, they are particularly appropriate in certain contexts.

- For example, you might consider beginning or ending an 'argue/persuade/advise' response with a rhetorical question:

> Is it ever acceptable to value animals more than humans? Animal rights activists would have us believe that there can never be any justification for making an animal suffer; yet for people in pain and dying, the loss of a few animals seems a small price to pay for a treatment or cure.

GOOD POINTS:
- The topic is brought into immediate focus.
- The reader is challenged to confront the central issue.

- You might also find it useful to end an 'explain' response with an exclamation:

> Swimming has done so many things for me: it keeps me healthy, keeps my head clear, gives me the opportunity to compete and win trophies and has led me to excellent friends. I love the sport!

GOOD POINTS:
- The concluding statement captures simply the writer's emotions, which the exclamation mark stresses.

CHECK YOURSELF QUESTIONS

Q1 Change the following simple sentences into complex and compound sentences, so the text sounds as if it comes from a speech made by a politician.

Include all the words provided, but you can alter the order of these ideas and add extra words as necessary.

> We knew nothing about the plans. The intelligence services told us nothing. They are very secretive. We could have issued warnings. It is all very sad. We apologise. We wish we could turn back the clock. That is simply not possible. We wish we could offer reasons. That is not possible either. We do know the people responsible will be found. You can be sure. They will have to explain their actions. Then we might all feel better.

Q2 Read this final paragraph, from a persuasive article, then add:
- an effective opening sentence
- an effective final sentence.

> We should all give more money to worthy causes. At times, it seems an unfashionable thing to do, but when you consider the impact a donation can have on people's lives, it is unforgivable that so many give so little. Those who are religious should be willing to support charities because that is what religion tells them to do; those who do not believe in a God but still care about others should also contribute; and the rest of society could give a thought to the fact that it could be they themselves who might need help some time in the future.

Answers are on page 155.

Punctuation

To obtain top marks, you need to use a range of punctuation. This means you will be expected to move beyond just full stops and capital letters.

Where it is appropriate, the examiner will expect you to use commas, apostrophes, question marks and exclamation marks, speech marks, brackets, dashes, ellipses, colons and semi-colons.

◎ Commas

■ Commas clarify texts by:

1. separating the items in a list:

    We have a first class health service, education system, defence force and parliamentary system.

2. adding clauses or phrases to a main sentence:

Although we sometimes doubt politicians, they are working, slowly and carefully throughout the years, to make our lives better, so we should respect them.

3. adding extra detail to a noun or pronoun:

The Prime Minister, whom some may not like, is supported by his ministers. They, each responsible for some area of policy, have a difficult life, which most would not envy.

◎ Apostrophes

■ Apostrophes are used to:

1. indicate possession:

If the 'owner' is singular, the apostrophe goes before the 's':

e.g. Europe's problems, my aunt's car

When the 'owner' is plural, the apostrophe goes after the 's':

e.g. football clubs' problems, programmes' music

2. show where there is an omission:

The apostrophe goes where a letter, letters or even a word has been removed:

e.g. Is not it? becomes Isn't it?; You are losing becomes You're losin'; 4 of the clock becomes 4 o'clock

Apostrophes are often wrongly used; you must be careful only to use them where they are needed.

◎ Question marks and exclamation marks

■ Particularly in an exam, many students forget to include question marks: remember to use one at the end of every question.

■ Other candidates use too many exclamation marks. They should only be used to highlight humour, or register strong or sudden feelings like anger, surprise or delight (see pages 70–71).

■ Notice how punctuation is used in this extract, in which a doctor explains how he struggles with difficult patients:

comma to separate the phrase adding information to the main clause

> You have to be firm with them. On one occasion, an old lady complained so much that I could stand it no longer. 'Problems?' I said. 'You think you have problems? You should try doing my job!'

question mark clarifies how he said the word

emotion registered by exclamation mark.

GOOD POINTS:

- The question marks indicate the doctor's frustrations, so that we sense his voice rising.

- The final exclamation mark suggests he has reached the end of his tether.
- Without the punctuation, it would not be possible to know how the doctor wants us to read the text.

He could appear quite calm if a comma and full-stops were substituted: 'Problems,' I said. 'You think you have problems. You should try doing my job.'

◎ Speech marks

■ Although you will not be producing a narrative in your exam, you might well wish to include elements of speech in any Section B response, so you need to be aware of the rules governing its punctuation.

If the speaker follows the words spoken, punctuate, close the speech marks, then use a small letter to continue.

If the speaker comes in the middle of one interrupted sentence, for the second half put a comma, open the speech marks, then use a lower case letter to continue.

> 'Are you well?' asked my mother.
>
> 'He looks strange,' said my father.
>
> I replied, 'I'm as well as could be expected, under the circumstances.'
>
> 'In that case,' said my mother, 'we can proceed.'
>
> 'But I don't want to go to the dentist,' I said. 'Can't it wait until next week?'

If the speaker comes first, put a comma, then open the speech marks and start with a capital letter.

If the person speaking is placed between two complete sentences, put a full stop before the second one, open the speech marks, then re-start with a capital letter.

GOOD POINTS:

- When punctuating speech:
  - the speech marks go around the words actually spoken
  - punctuation at the end of speech is placed before the final speech marks
  - there can be only one speaker per paragraph.

◎ Colons and semi-colons

- There are two main uses for colons:

  1. to **introduce a quotation**:
     As the Queen said only yesterday:
     'The commoners are not what they were in my father's time.'

  2. to **introduce a list**, following a general statement:
     This town can be proud of its heritage: the cathedral, the castle and its famous men and women who fought for what was right.

- Semi-colons have two main uses:

  1. to **separate two closely-related sentences**, giving a shorter pause than a full stop:
     I know we can win the cup; we have the talent and the ambition.

  2. to **separate the sections of a complicated list**:
     I love John because he's so good-looking; I love Zack because he's kind; and Ryan is especially special because of the size of his wallet.

- Writers use colons and semi-colons to help make ideas clear. This is an extract from a review of a book that relates what happened in the Second World War to pupils from Dame Alice Owen's School.

For the historian, as well as for the general reader, fascinating light is thrown on so much of what happened in those years: rationing, the Blitz, firewatching, the arrival of the Americans, the BBC (much of which was also evacuated to Bedford), music, comics. A whole chapter deals with agriculture; two dozen Owenians went off to join the drive to grow enough food on British soil to feed the nation.

colon introduces a list

semi colon separates two closely related ideas

✔ GOOD POINTS:

- The colon comes between the general statement and the list.
- The semi-colon links the Owenians to the chapter on agriculture, indicating it is about their activities.

◎ Brackets and dashes

- Brackets are usually used to offer readers a touch of additional information.

- For example, here Norman Mailer describes George Foreman when he fought Mohammad Ali for the world title:

> His hands lost no speed, his hands looked as fast as Ali's (except when he got hit) and his face was developing a murderous appetite.
>
> *The Fight*

- Sometimes brackets make the words in them seem like an actor's 'aside', used to suggest a reaction or emotion to the reader. Here, Mailer describes Ali with one of his followers:

> While he spoke, Ali put his hands on Bundini's head as if a crystal ball (a black crystal ball!) were in his palms; each time he would pat Bundini's bald spot for emphasis, Bundini would glare at the reporters like a witch doctor in stocks.

GOOD POINT:

- The repetition of 'crystal ball', with the addition of 'black' the second time, gives an impression of humour or wonder.

- Dashes can be used to fulfil the same functions, but can also serve to make information stand out. In this extract from *The Sun*, the sums of money are made to seem particularly significant:

> Billionaire Chelsea owner Roman Abramovich has bought himself a new toy – a £72 million yacht.
> The Russian oil tycoon – worth £3.5 billion – stunned onlookers when the 378ft craft put into the South of France last night.
>
> *Martin Wallace*

◎ Ellipses

- An ellipsis (...) can be useful to provide a number of effects:

  to create the idea that the situation will run on for ever:

  And so, the dynasty seems set to continue...

  or to give an aura of mystery:

  Who can say what terrors they must have witnessed...?

  or simply to allow the readers to decide for themselves what might fill the space:

  They laughed, they cried, and sometimes, when the night was dark, there were other, wilder emotions...

⚡ A* EXTRA

▸ With all these techniques, it is vital to use them selectively; over-use limits their effectiveness. Rather than impressing the examiner with a wide range of techniques, over-use makes it appear that you do not have a proper understanding of their functions.

CHECK YOURSELF QUESTION

Q Punctuate the following extract correctly. You will have to replace some of the full stops that have been used.

In your version, try to use:
- commas
- apostrophes
- question marks
- an exclamation mark
- speech marks
- brackets
- dashes
- an ellipsis
- a colon
- semi-colons.

> The problem for most single parents men and women is that they have so little time to do anything but care for their children and work. Days are all the same make what seem like endless meals clean and tidy the house work in an attempt to pay for next weeks food and get as much sleep as possible. Its a limited existence.
>
> But what can be done. There must be ways that these people can make their lives a little easier.
>
> As far as I am concerned said Mr Grayson who works for a government agency all we can do is make clear the benefits they can claim and offer wherever possible support workers to help them through. Then, it depends how the individual reacts.
>
> Locally a considerable amount of money has been put into the system to help single parents over £500,000 but it does not seem to have done the trick. Every single parent I spoke to was struggling. Perhaps Mr Grayson needs to come up with some more ideas.

Answer is on page 155.

Vocabulary

Whichever question title you choose in Section B, your vocabulary will need to be appropriate.

If, in addition, you can use language imaginatively, so that it seems original, you will be rewarded with high marks. Only wide reading can produce the breadth of vocabulary that gives real confidence, but there are some basic areas that can be improved, such as:
• discourse markers
• the use of imagery.

◎ Appropriate vocabulary

■ The vocabulary you use must be suited to purpose and audience.

So, for example, if you have to produce a letter to inform your school or college governors about problems, the language should be formal:

> It is with considerable reluctance that I have to bring this serious matter to your attention...

On the other hand, a letter which explains problems to a pen-friend might be informal:

> You will never guess what happened to me. It was some big deal at the time...

■ However, no matter what the task, an extensive vocabulary is required for a top grade. You should, therefore:

• avoid repetition and aim for variety

If, writing to the governors, you first used achievement, you might later use success as an alternative.
The letter to your pen-friend might use terrible, awful, tragic, shattering, criminal, drastic, mind-numbing or cataclysmic to describe something bad.

• avoid slang and colloquialisms generally, though they can be used sparingly in some informal responses

For example, it would not be appropriate to tell the governors that some of the dinner ladies are 'minging'; but that might be fine if you were writing to a friend. You should bear in mind, though, that the examiner is still looking at the breadth of your vocabulary, so you would also need to use a range of standard English words.

• use words appropriate to the context

If, for instance, you are writing about care for the elderly, you might use terms like social services, mobility allowances and primary care; a response dealing with educational matters might include phrases like continuing education, tertiary provision and academic and vocational courses.

◎ Discourse markers

■ In any response, you must use discourse markers to join paragraphs and ideas together. These might be:

• To order your ideas: e.g. Firstly... Secondly... Finally...; To begin with... Then... And, to top it all...

- to give reasons: e.g. *Consequently*; *Therefore*; *As a result*

- to offer alternatives: e.g. *On the other hand*; *Yet*; *Meanwhile*; *Nevertheless*

- to develop a train of thought: e.g. *What this means is...*; *Supporting this concept...*; *Taking this one stage further...*; *Because of this...*

and so on.

Check back to see how they were used in the session on Structure and Paragraphs, especially pages 66–67.

◎ The use of imagery

■ A striking use of imagery will attract the examiner's attention. This is likely to be particularly relevant to descriptive writing but can be used in the other forms of writing too.

■ Your marks will be higher if you can use effective **similes**, which make a comparison using 'like' or 'as', and **metaphors**, which state things that are not literally true.

For instance, if you were seeking to advise a cousin to stay on at university, you might use expressions like:

Although your father seems **as old-fashioned as a sideboard,** *in this case he is right...*

Your opportunity to work for that company might seem **like a ticket to paradise** *right now, but unless you complete your course...*

Even though **your lecturers come from the age of the dinosaurs,** *they can give you the opportunity to...'*

You exploded *when I last suggested this, but,* **at the risk of inviting another full-frontal attack,** *I must tell you again that...*

■ You can also impress by using **onomatopoeia** – where you capture sounds in words – and **alliteration**, where words that are close together begin with the same letter:

Imagine the dull thud as the university's door to opportunity closes behind you...

What a weary way *you will have to tread, without further qualifications...*

■ Such imaginative uses of language will enrich your response and gain marks.

'Even though your lecturers come from the age of the dinosaurs...'

CHECK YOURSELF QUESTION

Q Decide which discourse markers, similes, metaphors or appropriate
vocabulary might best fit into the following informative extract:

My life in the hospital kitchen is very different from my existence at school.
Within the ………. of day to day life at my 'centre of excellence', no one
bothers me. I can dream my hours away, gaze out of the window and
imagine………………………………………………………………………………………
……………………………………………………......

…………., it is very different when I am working in the evenings at the hospital.
As I slave in the pan room, over sinks of boiling water, there is no window.
There are cooking pots to scrub and I am like …………..: wash the pan, sterilise
it, leave it to drain, move on to the next. …………...… in school a teacher might
occasionally encourage me back to reality, in the steam of …………… I am
generally alone. There is just the intense heat, the sweat from my brow and the
………… of aluminium for hours on end. I feel like I am working ……………..
……………………………………………………………………………………………
……………………………………………………

Answer is on page 156.

WRITING SKILLS ◦ ◦ ◦ ◦ ◦ ◦ ◦ **79** ◦ ◦ ◦ ◦ ◦ ◦ ◦ ◦ ◦ UNIT 3

Spelling and accuracy

In Section B, accurate spelling is expected from top candidates. This is one reason why the exam paper recommends that you spend five minutes at the end checking and improving your writing.

Your writing also needs to be legible, and set out in an appropriate form.

Accurate spelling

- As you prepare for your exam, it is wise to look back through work that has been marked during the last two years. Note words you spelt incorrectly and make sure you can spell all of them correctly now. In addition, where words follow a set pattern, remember it so that you can spell other related words, or words affected by the same rule; for example:

  - words ending with a single vowel and single consonant double the consonant if you add an ending beginning with a vowel:
    sit – sitter – sitting; ban – banned – banner

  - remove the final 'e' from a verb before adding 'ing':
    love – loving; have - having

- Although you should never copy text from Section A, it often contains vocabulary that is useful for Section B. Make sure that you always spell correctly words included in the stimulus materials or on the examination paper itself.

Common errors

- There are some words which are used frequently by candidates but which cause spelling problems. You need to avoid the most common errors. In particular, know the difference between:

  your (belonging to) and you're (you are)

  their (belonging to), they're (they are) and there (any other use)

  where (place), were (verb) and we're (we are)

  too (as well or very), two (the number) and to (any other use)

Frequently used words

- Avoid further difficulties by making sure you can spell these words which are frequently used and which are also frequently mis-spelt:

argument	disappear	independent	professional
atmosphere	dynamic	metaphorically	psychological
beautiful	embarrassed	naïve	sense
beginning	emphasise	necessary	stereotype
business	empathise	occasionally	suspense
character	environment	parallel	symbol
conscience	favourite	persuade	unnatural
definitely	immediately	prejudice	vicious
develop			

⚡ A* EXTRA

▸ It is likely there are many words you, personally, use frequently. For example, you probably use the same discourse markers in most discuss/argue/persuade responses. Ensure you can spell them accurately.

◎ Checking and correcting

■ One of the most serious mistakes made by candidates is that they do not check and improve their writing. Failure to do so can affect your mark considerably, because vocabulary, punctuation and spelling can all be improved. Ideally, read through your response very slowly, as if reading aloud, and be prepared to alter your work whenever necessary.

■ With regard to spelling, check for:

  • words spelt differently in different parts of your answer: decide which version is correct

  • words which are clearly spelt wrongly: try to apply spelling rules.

■ Do not be afraid to make alterations. As long as the end result is legible, you will not lose marks. However, if the marker cannot make sense of what you have produced, that will let you down.

? CHECK YOURSELF QUESTION

Q   List all the errors in the article below and write the correct version of each word:

Why we should eat healthy food

People should except the arguement that eating healthy food is good for us. It makes our exsessive weight disapear and has a good sychologicle affect on our state of mind. It doesnt matter if we ocasionaly have a cake or some choclate, but we should definately eat fruit and vegatables every day and losts of fruit; that's the only way to improof ourselfs and our society.

We are lucky that today most people have enough money to buy descent things to eat, but instead they wast there money on burgers and chips. Parents should be embarassed too let it happen and childen should have more sence. I am hopeing that things will realy improve in our school, because the canteen is new and the food for sale is truely healthy.

Answer is on page 156.

TYPES OF WRITING

What you will be assessed on

Section B of both English examination papers will expect you to produce a Writing response. In both cases, you will have to choose one title from the four offered and you are recommended to spend 45 minutes on this section.

On Paper 1, there will be three titles, one asking you to argue, one to persuade, and one to advise. There will also be a title that will involve two or three of these approaches.

On Paper 2, there will be three titles, one asking you to inform, one to explain, and one to describe. There will also be a title that will involve two or three of these approaches.

The marks you receive will be awarded for the quality of your Writing skills. You will be assessed on
* communication and organisation
* sentence structure, punctuation and spelling.

◎ Sentence structure, punctuation and spelling

■ The previous section of this book deals with general writing skills, including how to vary your expression, sentences and vocabulary, and how to make your writing, including your spelling, as accurate as possible.

■ There is also more on Writing skills in this section, relating your skills to each type of writing.

See Writing Skills, Sessions 1-6
Types of Writing, Sessions 1-7

◎ Communication and organisation

■ The marks you receive for communication and organisation are given for the organisation of your ideas, your use of language and the fluency of your response. These qualities depend on the appropriateness of what you write: the way in which you target purpose and audience.

■ The purpose of your response will be to argue, persuade, advise, inform, explain or describe; and you will be expected to produce the form of writing that has been requested. This might be quite specific, especially for Paper 1. For example, you might be asked to write a letter, article or speech. For Paper 2, it is more likely that you will be asked to produce a standard 'essay'. In each case, the style you use must fit the task.

- The audience, the person or people for whom you are writing, may be of a certain age or from a certain background. You may be writing for senior citizens or school governors, for example. For Paper 2 in particular, you may be writing for the examiner. Again, it is essential that you use language and content that are suitable.

- The different kinds of writing may have common features: an introduction, conclusion and logical development in paragraphs; the use of quotations, anecdotes, humour and imagery.

- The following sessions deal with these features in detail, and you will see where they are particularly appropriate. In addition, there will be specific qualities which the examiners will be looking for in relation to the particular type of writing.

WRITING TO ARGUE

- If you write to argue, your response will be expected to include two opposing points of view: if you are arguing in favour of or against something, there must be a case to argue against.

- See Session 1

WRITING TO PERSUADE

- Persuasive writing can use argument, but that is not always necessary. Often, the persuasion can come from developing just one 'angle'. Also, it is common to use emotive approaches which touch the reader's emotions.

- See Session 2

WRITING TO ADVISE

- If you are advising someone, your response should be clear, logical and move to a definite conclusion. Advice is of little use if it is not convincing.

- See Session 3

WRITING TO INFORM

- Informative writing must give facts and relevant opinions. The information should be detailed and relevant.

- See Session 4

WRITING TO EXPLAIN

- When you write to explain, you are giving reasons, saying why or how something happens or happened. Rather than just providing information, you will be expected to give insight and explanation throughout.

- See Session 5

WRITING TO DESCRIBE

- The examiner will be looking for description, not narrative. In other words, you will be asked to describe a person, place or incident but are most unlikely to be asked to produce a story.

- See Session 6

BLENDING THE SKILLS

- If you choose the final question on the papers, you will have to blend your writing skills. So, for example, if you were asked to argue and persuade, your response should include both types of writing, and the same would be the case if you were required to inform, explain and describe.

- See Session 7

Writing to argue

Including two points of view

- An argument must have two sides. If there is no alternative viewpoint, there can be no argument. This means that when you write to argue you must always be aware of the opposite point of view and include it in your response.

- You can structure your ideas in a variety of ways. You might, for example:
  - decide to present one side of the argument, then put the alternative

  or
  - put one idea, then contradict it; present another, and contradict it, and so on

  or
  - make passing references to another viewpoint as you develop your own ideas.

- Consider how these extracts are presenting argument in different ways. They are both dealing with funding for schools.

TWO BALANCED SIDES

> According to our Head, the money we raise is vital for our school: it buys extra sports equipment, for example, and is helping to develop the fund that will buy a new minibus in two years. He tells us that without our raffle ticket sales, our craft fairs and coffee mornings, the school would be much worse off in so many ways. He also says we value our school more if we have contributed to its development.
>
> On the other hand, it seems that we concentrate more on raising money than on raising examination results. People are praised for their fund-raising instead of their intellectual development. The school seems to have its priorities all wrong. It is more important to do your homework than do a sponsored run. The government should fund schools properly.

One side of the argument set out in some detail

'According to our Head', 'He tells us' and 'He says' show these are not necessarily the writer's views

An alternative viewpoint

The writer's opinion given in short, definite sentences

GOOD POINTS:
- One side of the argument is presented in some detail, although it is made clear that this is the Head's viewpoint.
- The alternative viewpoint is given in the second paragraph, in short, 'punchy' sentences which make it clear this is the writer's viewpoint.

Anyone who knows anything about schools is aware that more money is needed, and that the extra books and equipment it can buy help teaching to improve and results to rise. If this were not the case, independent schools would charge less and do without their excellent facilities. The fact that they invest in the latest books and technology implies that such spending is necessary if they wish to maintain their reputation.

Of course, as the government points out, the quality of teaching is the most important element of any school. Yet, teaching must be better when every student has a book and does not have to share, or has a PC on which to access the internet. Adequate funding is vital if these goals are to be achieved.

Writer's own view clear

Reason for view explained

Example of independent schools to prove point

An alternative viewpoint put very briefly

Alternative immediately attacked through 'yet' connective

Writer's own beliefs stated strongly again

GOOD POINTS:

- There is only one, relatively brief, mention of the other side of the argument.
- The opposing viewpoint is immediately dismissed so that the writer's views can progress.

Structuring your response

- Whenever you write to argue, you will be expected to include:
  - an introductory paragraph which presents the topic and probably suggests your attitude to it;
  - an argument which develops logically and progressively;
  - a conclusion to sum up your opinion.

- You should follow this approach whatever you are asked to write: possibly a letter, an article or an argument with no specific audience, which means you are writing for the examiner.

INTRODUCTIONS

- Candidates working at **C grade** might begin their response with a very simple introduction. For instance, if they were asked to write an article for an employers' magazine, to argue for or against work experience, they might begin with very general comments:

In my opinion, work experience is a good thing. Some people argue that it is a waste of time, but I am going to show that it helps students get to know what real life is like. There are many things in its favour...

- However, **an** A/A* candidate would use a more imaginative opening, taking the opportunity to capture the examiner's attention:

> I am not afraid to admit that the idea of work experience terrified me. How would I cope with new people, a new working environment and having to get up at six o'clock each morning? Would the fortnight even be worthwhile? I guessed not, and feared I would be bullied, put upon and, frankly, bored for most of my time. I felt certain I would be better off learning maths in a classroom, rather than draining oil in the local garage.
>
> However, that was before I arrived; and how wrong I was...

short and effective opening sentence

touch of humour

challenging questions

sense of personal involvement, even in an argumentative response

change of viewpoint – and writer's attitude made clear

GOOD POINTS:

- The lively introduction, both personalised and gently humorous, is intended to make the reader want to go on reading the article.
- The style is appropriate for the purpose and audience: entertaining yet setting out to argue.
- The subject of the article – work experience - is mentioned immediately, giving focus to what will follow.

- The use of the writer's fears presents one side of the argument, but that aspect is soon discounted.
- The writer's viewpoint changes at the start of the second paragraph and will, presumably, introduce the arguments in favour of work experience, which are to come.

DEVELOPMENT

- As part of the planning, you should decide what arguments you intend to deal with, in what order you will handle them and in what depth. So, for example, the student who worked at the garage might decide to write about:

PLAN
para 2: what I learnt about working in the team
   co-workers/responsibilities/support and
   development
Para 3: how I enjoyed the range of tasks
   opportunity to dismantle engines/jobs in office/
   breakdown outings
Para 4: what I learnt that I would not have learnt at
school
   dealing with real problems/longer hours/few breaks
   of any kind
Para 5: minor problems I encountered
   health and safety/some exploitation?/butt of
   humour
Para 6: problems encountered by my friends
   bad bosses/boring work/unfriendly
   workmates/treated as children
Para 7: why it is an invaluable experience
   school is too protected/we will soon be in these
   environments/will have to work for 40-50 years
Conclusion: back to the start
   why it was so beneficial

positives are stressed

alternative viewpoint

an overview

GOOD POINTS:

- There is logic in the development:
   – what I got out of it
   – some of my problems
   – others' problems
   – why, nevertheless, it is valuable.
- Different viewpoints are included.
- The candidate is aware of an overall structure, since the conclusion indicates it will link with the opening.

CONCLUSION

■ The conclusion should summarise the views you have been expressing; it sums up your argument. It is worth remembering, too, that it is the last thing the examiner will read before awarding your mark, so if you can make it memorable you will benefit.

A C Grade candidate might write:

> So, when I looked back on the two weeks, I realised that the problems didn't mean I hadn't learnt a lot and enjoyed myself. It was a great experience and I feel that I am now better prepared for a working life. I would recommend work experience to anyone.

■ An A/A* candidate would provide a more original ending, which will stick in the memory and which links clearly to the tone and style of the beginning:

> So, incredibly, in just two weeks it was all over. I had no fears left and I had made good friends I was sorry to leave – even though I did have a lot of sleep to catch up on... Any problems were only minor. I loved almost every minute, learnt a great deal, and they have offered me a Saturday job. I now believe that work experience is a vital part of the KS4 curriculum. If it comes to a choice between doing maths or cleaning out a filthy sump, I've learnt there is no real comparison. After all, as Mick the manager said: 'You're better off with oil dribbling down your nose than getting square roots drilled into your head.' I can only agree. Roll on next Saturday!

summary of the experience

links back to opening

summarises argument

still a personal response

main conclusion stated

additional thought: humour again – and quotation

enthusiasm backs up argument expressed

GOOD POINTS:

- The ending of the argument is positive and enthusiastic, stressing the writer's viewpoint.
- The writer is still using high quality features to make the response memorable: humour, quotation, discourse markers ('So', 'After all') and a variety of sentences.
- The relaxed style is maintained, but there is appropriate vocabulary ('Mick the manager', 'sump'). It leads to a very definite series of short, powerful sentences at the end.

⚡ A* EXTRA

▶ High level responses demonstrate a mixture of writing skills. Notice how, here, the writer has used a range of advanced punctuation to impress: a colon, speech marks, commas used accurately, an ellipsis and an exclamation.

◉ Using a range of techniques

■ This letter, written by an A* candidate to a local council, argues that more needs to be done for hard-pressed local residents. It uses many of the techniques that examiners are looking to reward with a high grade. In this case, the audience is different and the intention is to argue forcibly and formally, without the attempt to entertain:

Dear Sir,

Does our city have to suffer from graffiti and litter and heaps of junk in the streets? Is there nothing that can be done? You collect our taxes and say you are concerned about our problems, but nothing ever seems to improve. I am tired of living in what amount to slum conditions on my housing estate, and I know that you can do something about it, if only you develop a will to fight for improvement and a positive drive to improve our quality of life.

Ironically, on a regular basis we receive your leaflets, telling us how our neighbourhoods are safer and cleaner and how new action schemes are making our lives better. But we do not recognise what you describe. When the mayor writes:

'We can celebrate, because independent studies have confirmed the improvements in the state of our environment...'

we are simply amazed. He seems to have no idea of what it is really like.

Of course, if you ever set foot outside the town hall and visited us, you would see the truth for yourself. We have bins unemptied, then tipped all over the pavements; there are abandoned cars, which often rust for months before they are removed, and which local teenagers delight in torching; and the walls are covered in obscenities which will not scrub away.

Naturally, such conditions encourage some people to add to the mess, and develop in others a mentality of despair. Only last week, I found the old lady who lives next door to me in tears, because her walls had been spray painted and a dead cat had been thrown into her porch. She called the police. There was nothing they could do. There seems nothing any of us can do.

rhetorical questions to challenge the reader

strong statement of the writer's viewpoint

topic sentences for each paragraph, indicating what it will be about

the council's different viewpoint

quotation used to illustrate exactly what the council is saying

opposing viewpoint dismissed

a touch of sarcasm/humour: 'if you ever set foot...'

discourse markers ('Of course', 'Ironically', 'Naturally') used to link ideas

extended list of complaints: sentence variety – earlier there are shorter, more abrupt sentences: 'But we do not recognise...'

anecdote: brief incident giving a vivid example of what is happening

short sentences indicate despair

> That is why I am writing directly to you to say it is time to act. The people in this city deserve better and it is up to you to provide it. You won our votes: it is time you set about winning our hearts.

links with opening

memorable last sentence

GOOD POINTS:

- The writer has introduced two viewpoints, structured the letter logically and linked the opening and ending.
- Sentences and vocabulary are varied.
- Topic sentences guide the reader effectively; discourse markers are used for smooth development; the quotation highlights one viewpoint; sarcasm is used to poke fun at the council; and an anecdote is used for illustration.

CHECK YOURSELF QUESTION

Q Write a well-structured response to the following title. Use:

- an effective structure
- different viewpoints
- appropriate techniques.

Title: Write an article for a local newspaper, arguing that your town, village or city needs improvement.

Answer is on pages 157–8.

Writing to persuade

Section B of Paper 1 will offer you the opportunity of writing to persuade.

If you write to persuade, you will need to:
- structure your ideas appropriately
- use a range of persuasive techniques, which may include:
  - emotive language
  - examples and anecdotes
  - rhetoric.

◎ Structuring ideas

- There are different ways of persuading people. You might, for example, persuade readers by presenting a logical argument. In that way, persuasion can be like writing to argue, and you could use similar techniques to those set out in the previous session.

- However, unlike argument, persuasion does not necessarily need to include more than one point of view. Rather than balancing contrasting ideas or ensuring that another viewpoint is included, persuasive writing often presents just one, subjective view of a subject. This is the approach we will focus on in this session.

- So, for example, if you were writing a letter to persuade an elderly relative to protect herself against dangers in the home, all you need to do is stress the need for more protection, rather than valuing what is already in place.

- Firstly, you need to put your ideas into a sensible order and extend them, so that one idea flows logically from the previous one:

PLAN
Intro: the need to be secure
   She is an important part of the family; her home is not as safe as it should be
Para 2: new measures needed to give protection against burglars
   Not even a chain on the door; needs modern locks, an alarm etc
Para 3: what the other problems are and how they can be solved
   Old gas appliances; no wiring checks for years; gas service can be arranged annually; local, friendly odd-job man will do the wiring
Para 4: the benefits which will come from greater protection
   She can be more relaxed; cheaper home insurance – and improvements are likely to cost very little in total
Conclusion: how everyone in the family will feel better knowing she is safe
   She has to be there to cook me tea whenever I'm passing!

⚡ A* EXTRA

▸ Even when planning, remember that original ideas will improve the quality of the final response. In this plan, there are already some original touches, such as the final comment about popping in for tea. This suggests that the writer will be appealing to her particular audience (an older relative) in a way that is likely to 'win her round', and persuade her to make changes.

GOOD POINTS:

- The plan sets out to persuade by detailing the current problems and then moving on to the benefits which would come from taking action.
- Extra persuasion comes, for example, by emphasising the fact it would not be expensive to be safer.
- The introduction stresses the dangers but the conclusion celebrates 'feeling better', so the persuasion has a clear direction.

◎ Emotive language

- Emotive language – language which affects the reader's emotions – is a most effective technique when writing to persuade. It can often be a more powerful tool than cold logic.

So, a **C grade candidate** producing an opening paragraph might write:

> Dear Grandma,
>
> I have been thinking about the fact that you are not as safe in your home as you might be. I do not want to worry you, but I am concerned that someone could break in or that you could be harmed by a fire. I am not even certain that your gas fires and cooker have been checked recently. If you follow my suggestions, though, I can guarantee you will be perfectly safe.

An **A* candidate** might persuade grandma to take the situation seriously by using an emotive approach:

> Dear Grandma,
>
> I hope you are really well and not getting too involved in snowball fights this winter! I like to think of you safe in your flat, comfy in your armchair with the heating on, protected from the howling wind outside. In fact, we need to know you are secure and away from everything dangerous, because you have a wide family that loves you and needs you. Who could we find to make us special Christmas cakes if anything happened to you?

humorous opening, but appropriate for this audience

emotive details

touching sentiments

humour to balance the sentiment and the suggestion of possible dangers

GOOD POINTS:

- It uses emotive language (describing grandma in the flat and the family's feelings for her).
- It uses a tone which is appropriate for the audience: humorous and caring.
- It includes persuasion from the start: grandma must become more secure so the family feels better. Rather than worrying her, the letter is persuading her to do this for others.

◎ Examples and anecdotes

- Examples and anecdotes – extended examples, short stories which can be used to illustrate a point – can enrich your response by giving what you say more credibility. The reader is more likely to be persuaded if you can write about what has actually happened. You will be more convincing.

When writing about how grandma's current security measures offer only limited protection, a C grade candidate might write:

> You need to have more security around you to be safe. At present, you are vulnerable to thieves, because anyone could break in. That would be terrible, and you might never get over it. I cannot beg you enough to improve the security you have.

An A* candidate, on the other hand, would add more detail and a persuasive anecdote:

> Just think what you need, to be able to sleep soundly at night: new door locks, a chain on your front door, and, ideally, some sort of alarm. Dad fitted these as soon as we moved into our new house and we felt better immediately. You don't have these items at the moment, and it could cause you major problems. It was only last year that my friend's parents woke up to find a burglar crouched in their bedroom like a panther ready to strike. It terrified them. Like yours, their house doesn't have an alarm and I couldn't bear the idea of you ever having to suffer like that!

details of what is lacking: moves beyond the general to the specific

example of benefiting

the anecdote brings the possible repercussions into striking focus: and it will have considerable impact

emotive language again

✓

GOOD POINTS:

- The details clarify the problem (whereas the first example merely said 'you need to have more security').
- A simple example illustrates the benefits.
- The anecdote is appropriately brief but includes a powerful simile: it develops and illustrates the point being made.
- The anecdote does not disrupt the flow of the response, which can move on to the next point.

◉ Rhetoric

■ Rhetoric is 'language used for effect'. It can transform a promising response into one which deserves a top grade. Notice how these conclusions differ. The first is from a C grade candidate and the second from an A* candidate:

> If you go ahead and improve all these security measures, you will be much safer. Not only that, we will all feel better able to sleep at night, knowing you are safe. I hope you will believe what I have said, and make changes in the near future.
>
> Love...

> As far as the family is concerned, you are as valuable as the Koh-i-noor diamond and should be protected with even more care. We want you safe from burglars; we want you safe from all other dangers; we want you safe and with us for a very long time to come. It makes sense, grandma: when we consider the range of horrendous accidents and appalling assaults on people and property that take place daily, it has to be wise to take every available precaution. And, after all, is there any reason why you should not make all these improvements straight away? Don't forget, you have to be perfectly safe so you can cook me my tea whenever I'm passing!
>
> All my love...

figurative language: simile emphasises love
<u>repetition</u> to hammer home the points
elaborate language gives the impression that the writer has command of language and, by implication, the ideas
<u>rhetorical question</u> to challenge the reader
humour again to conclude

GOOD POINTS:

- A range of techniques is being used.
- As well as the rhetoric, there is a direct appeal to the reader.
- The writer, having used elaborate language, still returns to humour at the end, since this is appropriate for the old lady who will be receiving the letter.

Obviously, rhetoric is likely to be used throughout the response – not merely to create an effective conclusion!

⚡ A* EXTRA

▸ Remember that the quality of your vocabulary is always assessed, so even if you are writing for someone in the family, make sure you show a range of expression. Here, for example, there is the *Koh-i-noor diamond*; and there is alliteration (*appalling assaults on people and property*).

Using a range of techniques

■ Blending the various techniques dealt with in this session, an A* candidate produced this response to the following title:

Write an article for a national newspaper persuading more people to vote.

Why everyone should vote...

How many times have you heard people criticise the government? How many times have you heard someone at the bus stop moaning about taxes or transport or wars? And how many times have you heard people saying they don't vote anyway, because it does no good? As far as I am concerned, if they do not vote, they do not have any right to complain. More importantly, they are wasting a right. This right is beyond value. It is as simple as that.

Consider those who are oppressed around the world. They would give almost anything to be allowed to caste a vote for what they believe in. They are sent to prison for having an opinion, are tortured because they speak out, and often die like slaughtered animals because, quite simply, they do not have our democracy.

In contrast, so many people in the western world choose, blindly, to ignore the ballot box, claiming that it is a pointless exercise which makes no difference to the standard of their lives. They say their cross is meaningless, as if the very act of voting fritters away the time when they could be watching television or playing darts over a pint. They seem to have no perception of what matters. Martyrs have given their lives so that we might have a say in our own futures, but that means nothing to so many.

A recent television programme looked at two different democracies. It focused on a man in Africa who queued for ten hours to vote – it was the first time he had ever been able to. It also interviewed a Scottish man who had no plans to vote at all; he said he had never voted. The contrast was glaring. In our comfortable world, we seem to have lost our sense of values.

Yet, we must vote, because nothing is more important than the society in which we live, since that affects everything else in our lives. So, when the next election comes around, you should find the time to write your cross because it is not meaningless – it represents your right to choose. You should vote if you care about our country, and it will also help you justify your protests afterwards.

rhetorical questions and repetition create a challenging opening

clear point of view: hammered home by short sentences

examples: emotive images and simile

elaborate language suggests knowledgeable writer

alternatives trivialised

emotive

anecdote highlights main point of article

unremitting persuasion

links back to opening

GOOD POINTS:

- The text is persuasive throughout.
- The full range of techniques is used effectively.
- There is a powerful opening and the conclusion links back to it.
- Sentences and vocabulary are varied.

? CHECK YOURSELF QUESTION

Q Write the script of a talk to be given on radio, to persuade the listeners to become more involved in helping charities.

Make sure you structure your talk effectively, and include:
- emotive language
- at least one example and anecdote
- rhetoric.

Answer is on pages 158–9.

Writing to advise

If you choose not to write to argue or persuade on Section B of Paper 1, the alternative is writing to advise.

Effective advice involves:
- the appropriate sequencing of your ideas
- being logical
- adopting the right tone
- offering reasoned solutions
- using examples.

Sequencing

■ There are two methods you can employ when organising your ideas on any particular subject. You might decide to:

1. set out a problem in considerable detail, then offer advice in the later part of the response:
   e.g. in an article in a magazine for teenagers:
   - page one explains how problems with parents can become very serious
   - the second page gives advice about how to avoid or minimise any such problems.

or:

2. offer advice as you detail the problem(s), so the advice is interspersed with the problems:
   For example:
   The first thing you mention in your letter is... I think that you need to tackle this in three different ways...
   You then go on to explain that... In this particular case, you might consider...
   Then, there is your concern about... If I were you, I would...

■ Both approaches are perfectly valid; but the way you decide to structure your advice will obviously influence your planning.

Being logical

■ Your advice is unlikely to be convincing if it is not logical. That means you need to:

1. show exactly what the problem involves

2. explain what can or should be done about it, making sure that your ideas have an obvious connection and are a sensible development from the problem(s) you have set out.

■ The final stage might well be to show what will be the benefits if your advice is followed.

■ When asked to write a section of the school brochure, to offer advice about settling in for new students arriving at her school, a candidate produced this plan:

PLAN
Intro: outline of all the trickiest problems
   complicated timetable, big school, confusing layout, moving
   each lesson, carrying books, masses of students and teachers
Para 2: how to understand the timetable
   why it's necessary, making effective use of student planner
Para 3: how to find your way around
   map in planner and on corridors, signs on walls, asking for help,
   subject areas

Para 4: how to cope with so many books
rucksack/locker, bringing what's needed just for
the day
Para 5: how to cope with students
avoid bullies, get help from form tutor, try to stick
with one or two friendly students at first
Para 6: how to cope with teachers
obey the rules, show respect and honesty
Conclusion: how to be happy
be patient; integrate into the traditions of the school;
show students and teachers the same respect they
show you

GOOD POINTS:

- There is a logic to the structure: problems are briefly outlined in the introduction; each one is then expanded in a subsequent paragraph.
- Advice is offered at each stage ('how to...' being the repeated phrase).

⚡ A* EXTRA

▸ On occasions, your advice can be made more effective by explaining what might happen if:
- nothing is done
If you just turn up and expect everything to be fine, you will struggle. If you do not adopt a positive attitude...
- your advice is ignored in favour of another approach
Some others will tell you to just follow what your friends do – whatever they do. However, that can lead to disaster...

◉ The appropriate tone

- As with any other response, the tone is dependent on the purpose and audience.

- There is always likely to be a degree of formality in what you are asked to write – so you are more likely to be asked to write a letter to a newspaper than to your best friend.

- You need to address the reader appropriately from the outset.

- This C grade response chooses to start with imperative verbs which instruct the reader about what to do; they are often a feature of good advice:

> Do not worry when you come to our school. You must get to grips with a whole new situation, including the crowds, the size of the school and all the new people. You should take a deep breath and must not panic. Keep your cool. You will soon get used to it all.

- However, this A* candidate blends the imperatives with a less aggressive approach:

GOOD POINTS:

- The imperatives also offer clear advice.
- The less aggressive approach in the A* response is likely to make the newcomer more confident: the tone implies throughout that the writer understands the situation of the newcomer and is clearly sympathetic ('everyone has been new at some stage').
- The A* response is more detailed and, therefore, more convincing.

> When you first arrive at our school, the best thing to do is to try not to panic. Everyone has been new at some stage. If you can stay calm, then you will be on the way to coping with your new world. See the long corridors as a challenge; see the complex timetable as a puzzle; and see the students and teachers as friends-to-be. Don't worry if your bag is too heavy or you have no idea what to do next. Think back to how frightening your primary school seemed at first. You soon got used to it, and the same will happen here.

UNIT 4 ○ ○ ○ ○ ○ ○ ○ ○ ○ ○ ○ ○   96   ○ ○ ○ ○ ○ ○ ○ ○   TYPES OF WRITING

◎ Offering solutions

- This response has been structured in sections so that a solution can be offered to each particular problem. Each section requires, therefore:
  - an explanation of the problem
  - advice to solve it, with an explanation of why it will be effective.

A C grade candidate is likely to deal with this in a relatively simple manner:

> You will have to cope with strange lesson times, which vary each day. I suggest you always wear a watch, because that will help you to avoid becoming totally confused. The timetable in your planner gives you the times of each lesson, so you will know exactly where you ought to be and when.

- This advice is somewhat limited and, although the reader can work out the significance of the watch, there has to be some 'reading between the lines'.

This A* extract is much clearer and more logical:

> Because the lesson times vary so much, at first it is difficult to know exactly how the school timetable operates. I recommend you always keep your planner with you, because that lists all the important times in the school day, so you can use it for reference whenever it is needed; and, in addition, try to go through it each evening, to remind yourself of what will be happening tomorrow. Then, provided you wear a watch, there should be few serious problems: check the planner, check your watch, and you will be able to arrive where you need to be - on time and with no stress at all.

GOOD POINTS:

- The problem, solution and explanation are all made clear.
- What needs to be done seems straightforward and appears a logical solution: use the planner and the watch.
- The advice is comforting, suggesting this is not a serious problem and if the advice is followed the problem disappears.

◎ Using examples

- Often, advice can prove more acceptable if it can be related to what has happened previously:
  - 'Consider what happened when…'
  - 'It is worth remembering…'
  - 'In a similar situation…'
  Such advice makes the reader feel there is less risk in what is offered. It seems easier to trust.

Look at the differences between the first conclusion, written by a C grade candidate, and the second written by an A* candidate:

> If you accept the advice offered in this booklet, you should be fine. You can look forward to a happy school career, because you will have got most of the problems sorted out already. However, don't come to the school half-heartedly. Make every effort to blend in, work hard and your future should be rosy.

You can look forward with confidence to a happy future at this
school. Other students who have followed this advice have settled down
within a week or so. As one said last year: 'I've only been here two
weeks, and it feels like home already.' All you need to do is what
others have done before you: integrate into our ways of working, and
give other students and teachers the respect you expect yourself. You
will have a wonderful time.

Welcome from us all.

GOOD POINTS:

The first example:
- offers a conclusion that has
  some enthusiasm ('your
  future should be rosy')
- but is not totally convincing
  ('should be' is repeated).

The second example:
- looks back to previous
  successes

- ends by implying the advice is
  easy to follow and it need not
  be a traumatic introduction to
  the school ('All you need to
  do is…')
- summarises the body of the
  response
- gives a conclusion which,
  because of the examples and
  the sensitive approach, makes
  the advice much more likely
  to be accepted.

◎ Using a range of techniques

- Blending the various skills dealt with in this session, an A* candidate
  produced this response to the following title:

  Write an article for a travel magazine, to advise travellers on
  how to cope with foreign languages.

Traditionally, the British speak English and expect the rest of the world
to adapt accordingly: if some foreigner does not speak English, then shout
at him, and he will get the idea! However, although that has often been
the attitude in the past, the world has moved on; and, thankfully, so has
the British attitude to travel and languages.

Most of the British who go abroad now realise that, to get the most out
of their time, they need to be able to 'speaka de lingo' – or, at least,
some of it. They can then get on better with the locals, pick up a
clearer flavour of the culture and feel as if they have really been somewhere
foreign, not just a Brighton with endless sunshine. They can feel less
like holidaymakers and more like travellers.

Of course, it is hard to suddenly just be there and 'talking the talk', so
sensible travellers do a little work at home. Language guides, in either
book or tape form, give an excellent start. It is amazing how your
attitude can change when you realise it is so simple to ask for bread or
to order a drink in the language of your choice. My brother, who is only

seven, loves being in Paris because he can go out each morning to the bakery with his 'Je voudrais une baguette, s'il vous plaît.' He hands over his euro and comes back smiling, having done himself good and also having done something positive for Anglo-French relations.

Unfortunately, it is far too easy to settle for a handful of phrases when you are away, and to fail to develop your language skills any further. We encounter so many foreigners who can speak English so well, we fall into the trap of relaxing totally, and fail to add to our new vocabulary. In such circumstances, we are the losers.

So, we should be learning from the signs around us, from menus and just from what we hear in the street. Also, your hosts will be delighted if you ask what they call knives and forks or razor blades or lipstick. They will even teach you whole sentences once you show an interest – and it is incredible how swiftly you will 'pick it up'. Kein problem, as we say in German.

It is simply a matter of making the effort and then appreciating the results. Travel broadens the mind and, if the experience can also extend your language skills, the journey has been doubly worthwhile.

anecdote to prove the point

French used for illustration

positive results

possible pitfall: problem

effect if we fail to act

advice again

appropriate examples

German used for illustration

persuasive conclusion, to make the advice more acceptable

GOOD POINTS:

- The response presents situations, offers advice and suggests likely outcomes.
- The tone is light – using other languages for illustrative purposes – but presents some serious points.
- The examples and anecdotes give the advice more credibility.

- The introduction is memorable, with the image of 'traditional' British behaviour.
- The response develops logically, leading to a much more positive conclusion.
- Language is used effectively – for example, 'amazing' to suggest that using other languages can be a thrill, and the use of 'simply' at the beginning of the final paragraph, to suggest that the remedy is not difficult.

? CHECK YOURSELF QUESTION

Q On behalf of your year group, write a letter to your headteacher to offer advice on how your school should spend a grant of £100,000, which has just been received from the government.

Answer is on pages 159–160.

Writing to inform

In Section B of Paper 2 one question will expect you to write to inform.

Writing to inform requires:
- the provision of information
- logical organisation
- the use of facts and opinions
- appropriate clarification
- a personal response.

◉ Providing information

■ The first, and most obvious, requirement of this type of writing is that information should be provided. However, to achieve a high grade you need to show that you can write in depth about the subject given, so it is not just a matter of setting down as many relevant ideas as you can. Rather than just providing an extended list, try to focus on the most significant points and include as much detail as possible.

■ Of course, you are likely to begin by collecting a range of relevant ideas, as in the spider diagram below in response to the question:

Write a letter to a pen friend who is about to visit, to inform them about the area in which you live.

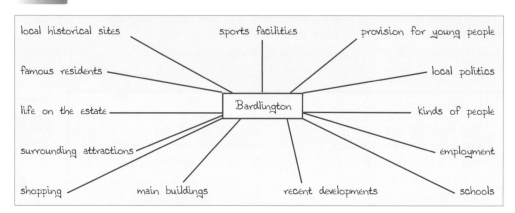

local historical sites — sports facilities — provision for young people — famous residents — local politics — life on the estate — Bardlington — kinds of people — surrounding attractions — employment — shopping — main buildings — recent developments — schools

All these ideas are relevant, but it would then be necessary to decide which ones you could deal with in the time allowed.

◉ Logical organisation

■ Whenever you produce a written response, your ideas should develop logically, so that one point appears to develop from what has gone before, and this letter should be no different. The detailed plan requires logical progression:

PLAN

Intro: general details
  looking forward to the visit, much to
  find out about, many things to see   *introduction gives summary*

Para 2: immediate vicinity   *begins close to home*
  neighbours, the estate – shops and
  houses

Para 3: the town   *broadens scope to wider town*
  employment, schools, facilities

Para 4: what's worth seeing   *further step to significant buildings etc*
  historical sites, buildings, attractions

Para 5: other points of interest   *then mentions other interesting features*
  youth culture, recent improvements

Conclusion: summary of Barlington   *concludes with personal response*
  some fun, some interest

◎ Facts and opinions

- The information you supply is almost always likely to be a mixture of facts and opinions.
  - The facts provide the substantive detail.
  - The opinions provide an assessment of the material, and can give it a more personal focus.

- Even an introduction is likely to combine these features. Notice how, in these examples, the second response, from an A* candidate, provides a more distinct 'angle' on the local environment than the first C grade reponse:

> Dear Gabbi,
>
> We are looking forward to your visit and you will be with us soon. I thought I would tell you something about where we live so you will know what to expect when you arrive. I hope you are going to have a good time, because there are many things to do and see.

> Dear Gabbi,
>
> I imagine you are starting to worry about what your two weeks with us might bring. So, to set your mind at rest, I thought I would tell you all about our little community, so there will be no unexpected surprises when you arrive. There are many positives: we are surrounded by bits and pieces of history, which can be quite fascinating. Also, there are some unusual aspects: some of the families who live around us lead very odd lifestyles- but they aren't dangerous!

◎ Appropriate clarification

- When you write to inform, it is essential that you make the information clear. Usually, the reader will not be aware of the situation, place or whatever is being described. You should not, therefore, assume the reader has knowledge.

- The letter to Gabbi needs to be absolutely clear, because she probably has no prior knowledge of the local area.

> There are many things worth seeing locally, if you are interested in things like history. There is a civil war castle that is still just about standing and the town hall and the county hall are both in town and quite grand. They have big pillars outside and are next to the law courts. We might also go to the boating lake, where we will be able to hire a canoe, and there is a reservoir, if you like walking round in a circle, just to get back where you started.
>
> I think you might be more interested in our youth club...

limited vocabulary ('things')

relevant , but lacking detail

jumbled ideas (what is the connection between the pillars and the courts?)

again, these are relevant details but need clarification: where are these attractions, how big are they, and so on?

good link to next paragraph and the opinion is clear: probably indicating this is what the writer finds more interesting!

We do have, though, some attractions which you are likely to find genuinely interesting. For a start, my parents intend to take us to the castle, which is only a couple of miles away and in all the history books. It was the site of a famous battle during the wars of the Roses (1460) and besieged several times during the Civil War (1642-48). From the top, you get panoramic views of the countryside around, and can imagine the clashing of swords and cries of the dying men as the relatively primitive armies struggled, fought hand to hand and wreaked massive devastation. The museum on site exhibits many of the weapons and has detailed charts of how the battles were organised...

links with previous paragraph
personal opinion

detailed clarification

personal response creates a vivid impression of the castle

assured language

further detail

▶ Each of the A* extracts in this session has included appropriate personal response from the writer. This lifts the material from being just itemised details, and reveals a critical awareness: whether things are of value and why (for example: *you can imagine the clashing of swords...*).

GOOD POINTS:

- The detail, personal response and mature language bring the attraction to life.
- The paragraph has been linked to what preceded it.

◉ Personal response

■ Although not all tasks are the same, a personal response is also likely to be a significant feature of most conclusions, because at this point you are summing up for the reader and, hopefully, giving perspective to what you have been informing them about.

The personal response might be relatively simple, as in this C grade response:

You should now have a good picture of what it is like here, and we hope you will have a wonderful time whilst you are with us. You will be able to experience the things I have told you about, and give us your opinions on them. Personally, I am certain you will enjoy the sports facilities best – but we will see whether I am right.

Best wishes...

On the other hand, it might be more striking as in this A* grade response:

The one certainty is that you will be given the warmest of welcomes and I can promise you a variety of experiences: fascinating guided tours of our historical heritage; exhausting afternoons playing squash at the sports centre; and hysterical evenings with my crazy friends. I am intending to give you a thoroughly 'English' experience. In fact, whatever else happens, before you go home you will be treated to a huge helping of local fish and chips, which we can eat out of newspaper – and that should give you something to remember when you return to your bistros and cafes!

Best wishes...

personal response throughout the paragraph, and from the start

cluster of informative detail, with opinions included ('exhausting', 'hysterical')

final example of what the area has to offer

personal opinion on the effect it will have

GOOD POINTS:

- The response is still informative.
- Personal opinion is promoting a positive response to what the writer is offering – suggesting it will all be enjoyable.
- The sentences are varied and the use of language is imaginative (e.g. 'historical'/'hysterical')
- The letter draws to an effective ending, introducing fish and chips as the climax and then imagining the guest returning home.

Using a range of techniques

■ Employing informative writing techniques effectively, an A* candidate produced this response to the following title:

Write an article for a national broadsheet newspaper, to inform the readers about the problems faced by modern teenagers.

It has never been easy to be a teenager, and it is particularly difficult today. The world expects us to be grown up but rarely treats us like adults; we are part of a society in which drugs are readily available but extremely dangerous; our education consists of examinations and more examinations; and, on top of that, we have the perennial problems of adolescence, as we cope with so many changes and try to come to terms with our new selves. Is it any wonder we struggle at times?

One of the biggest problems is that parents and teachers demand mature and intelligent behaviour from us, yet usually think of us as still being children. We help clean the house, do a range of chores and care for sickly grandparents, but cannot watch adult movies on television. We are expected to show an interest in current affairs and get a part-time job to begin to support ourselves, but are not even allowed a say in where we go for the family holiday – never mind being allowed to holiday with our friends!

immediate link with title complex sentence informs reader of the range of problems

rhetorical question implies personal response

paragraph linked

detailed information on home life

problems apparent

again, a personal 'slant' on the situation

Outside the home, we have to make sure our dissatisfaction does not lead us to outright rebellion and to the dealers who are just waiting to sell us a myriad of drugs. Older generations had to come to terms with alcohol and cigarettes; that was easy, by comparison. We go to a club, to dance, then are faced with temptation, peer pressures and our own desire to fit in with the crowd. There is always someone there with a baseball cap, a designer smile and the latest designer drug to tempt us. Being a teenager has never been harder.

Of course, it has never been so grim in school either. We have so many examinations, it is difficult to keep track: SATs, GCSEs, A/S levels... and the practice tests that accompany them. Homework is never-ending. No teacher seems aware of how much work the others are setting, and, anyway, would not care, because they are all under orders to improve results or their own careers will suffer.

Through all this, teenagers are suffering from raging hormones, relationship problems, changes in their bodies and their minds and the fear of suddenly being alone. They are no different, in that sense, from their parents and grandparents. But would previous generations have wanted all the other modern pressures? I imagine they feel fortunate to have been born at another time, in another world.

links again

vocabulary impressive throughout

'designer': repeated modern word emphasises modern problem

personal comment

linked once more

detailed information on problems of school life

vocabulary impresses: mature for national broadsheet

cluster of problems to conclude

rhetorical finish puts all the information into perspective

GOOD POINTS:

- The writer presents organised and detailed information.
- The facts are supported and illuminated by opinions.
- The language and style are mature and appropriate for the given purpose and audience.

CHECK YOURSELF QUESTION

Q   Write informatively about a pastime you enjoy.

In a task of this kind, you should assume your audience is the examiner.

Answer is on pages 161–2.

Writing to explain

One of the questions in Section B of Paper 2 will offer you the opportunity to write to explain. If you choose that title, you need to be aware that explanation is different from straightforward information.

Writing to explain requires:
- a response which answers the precise demands of the title
- content which sets out how or why something occurs, rather than just what happens
- appropriate language.

◎ Responding to the title

■ Many candidates in the examination fail to explain properly the subject about which they are writing. It is easy to lose focus and just write to inform, without including the explanation that is required.

Think about this title:

Most people have memories of a particular holiday or trip. Choose one that you have experienced, and explain why it was so memorable.

It does **not** ask you to:
- write about trips in general
- describe what happened on one special trip
- write informatively about the place you visited.

It **does** require you to:
- decide what made one particular trip special and say why
- select memorable features of the trip and explain why they are memorable.

■ For a high level response, you need to limit the points about which you are writing, explaining them at length, rather than trying to include too much material. This is another instance when it is better to write a lot about a little, rather than to write a little about a lot!

So, your plan might look like this:

PLAN
Intro: where we went, when, why memorable
    Turkey, highs and lows
Para 2: first part fun
    different culture, beaches, food, friends: show why
Para 3: dad's nightmare
    drunken evening, people complaining, wrestling with red monster: explain what happened
Para 4: mum bitten by cat
    rabies fears, doctor and hospital, injections: how the horror unfolded
Para 5: leaving
    friendliness: doctor and nurses: explain it still didn't take away the horror
Conclusion: never going back!
    problems outweighed pleasures

GOOD POINTS:
- There is clear organisation: the introduction sets out to show two sides to the holiday, which are exemplified in the sections which follow and are balanced in the conclusion.
- The concept of 'explain' is maintained throughout: 'why', 'explain', and 'how' are all important words in this plan.

- It is wise to explain from the beginning of the response. It establishes your focus, which is then easier to maintain.

Look at how these C grade and A* grade candidates approach the task differently:

> About six years ago, I went on holiday with my family to Turkey. We stayed in a place called Datca, and there were not many British people there. I am sure we could have had a good time and then it would have been 'just another holiday'. However, there were also some seriously bad moments which made the holiday especially memorable.

> When it comes to memorable holidays, our family's package expedition to Datca in Turkey will take some beating. We had a beautiful place to stay in a resort which is lovely, and all of that is captured in our photographs – yet that summer stands out because of one particular experience, which we did not record on camera but which we will never forget. It has haunted us ever since.

A* EXTRA

▸ You should always bear in mind that the examiner is looking to reward language competence, so sentences with varied length and structure – such as these – will create a positive impression.

GOOD POINTS:

The A* opening:
- is more detailed
- immediately introduces more vivid explanation – the experience which 'has haunted us ever since'
- has more varied sentences.

◎ 'How' and 'why'

- Good explanatory writing presents a situation, then says why it came about and the effect it had. Sometimes, depending on the title, it might explain how someone feels about what has happened. Throughout, it gives reasons.

Look at how the middle section of the response can be improved from a C grade ...

informs about what happened and the consequences

explains the effect on the family

links to title: explains why it has made such an impression

> My mother had a real problem. One night, she was bitten by a cat. She had to go to see the doctor and then to the local hospital, where she was told she had to have an injection into her stomach every two days. They thought she might have rabies. This was terrible, and made our holiday a nightmare. My mother was really frightened, and cried quite often. The injections really hurt her, and it is not something we will ever forget.

Incredibly, though, something even worse happened to my mother. My father's problems caused us unforgettable embarrassment, but my mother's misfortune turned our holiday into a nightmare – one from which we could not wake up.

It all started when my mother was bitten by a cat. She was eating in a restaurant and moved her arm suddenly and a cat, which was beside her chair and must have thought she was going to harm it, struck first. The doctors feared she might have rabies. This meant she had to have a series of six injections directly into her stomach – one every two days. As you can imagine, our holiday was wrecked. The injections caused agony, she spent much of the day in tears, her stomach became black and swollen and all we could do was watch her suffer. It was no longer a holiday but a daily torture for everyone.

links with previous paragraph
explains why these incidents were memorable
echo of 'haunting' from introduction

candidate has decided to use an extra paragraph, to properly detail what happened

explains how this affected them

further information
further explanation of effect

GOOD POINTS:

The A* extract:
- links clearly to the previous paragraph about the father
- offers more detail and more explanation
  – clearly explains the incident, concentrating on how it came to affect the family so much and why it is, therefore, so memorable
  – brings the incident vividly to life ('her stomach became black and swollen')
  – develops the response beyond the original plan. It is not changed, but expanded, using two paragraphs, since the incident is crucial to why the holiday has been especially memorable – the first of these two paragraphs can then give a startling explanation and the second expand on it.

⚡ A* EXTRA

> It is, obviously, unwise to ignore your original plan: that means the planning time has been wasted. However, it is sometimes possible to develop one paragraph into two, in order to achieve a particular effect. You might wish, for instance, to produce a one-sentence paragraph, such as:
> *She could not stand it any longer and she collapsed in hysterics.*
> As long as you then go back to your planned structure, all will be well.

◎ Using appropriate language

■ It is important that the explanation is clear, so that the reader understands it perfectly. There is a range of explanatory phrases you are likely to find useful in many responses. You can use:

1. terms to explain cause and effect, as you move from information into explanation

   As a result of this...   This meant that...
   This is because...   The reason for this...
   As a consequence...   Therefore...

2. modal verbs, when something is uncertain

   It could be...   It may be/might be that...

Some of these phrases have been used in this A* conclusion:

It might be that what happened to my mother has coloured my impressions of Turkey for ever. It is certainly a beautiful country, I know that; and it has wonderfully friendly people. However, my mother had a terrible time, my father was distraught for her, and the rest of us just felt helpless. This meant that things we might have enjoyed, like the beach, were just stops along the way to the next injection; and things we might have laughed at, such as my father's experience, pale into relative insignificance. My mother was in pain, and therefore we remember that above all else. It is a holiday we cannot forget - but for many of the wrong reasons.

modal verb

explains again why it was so memorable

cause and effect identified

still explaining how they were affected

GOOD POINTS:

- The holiday is effectively summarised.
- The effects of the misfortune are explained: we know why it was so memorable and how they reacted.
- 'It might be' and 'This meant that' helpfully support the explanation.

◎ Using a range of techniques

■ This A* response shows how to explain effectively, developing significant points, saying how and why things happened and using mature and assured language. The question asked candidates:

What do you dislike most about television?

I am sure that television is not all bad. It has educational uses, brings top sporting events into the living room and has the potential to enliven dark winter evenings. However, the diet that is drip-fed into my house does anything but stimulate the brain or delight the senses: it could cause premature aging and certainly hardens the arteries. I am sick of soaps, reality television and almost all things American.

I am going to ignore daytime television, since it is beneath contempt - but even in the evening there seems to be no originality at all in most of the programming. The soaps drip on, like some twenty-first century water torture. Everyone spends each evening in the pub; every community is afflicted by ever more incredible calamities; and we sit on our settees drinking our tea, eating our crisps and lapping up such rubbish, because there seems to be no alternative.

begins with positives, which then highlight what is wrong

contrast: explains what he dislikes most

exaggeration for effect

'sick' concludes imagery of food and eating

arresting simile

explains problems with evening TV

how we react and why

Actually, that is not totally true, of course. The twenty-first century has brought something new and different. Unfortunately, it is even more dire: the reality show. Because they are starved of anything better, and because the newspapers comment on these day after day, people sit and watch has-been semi-celebrities swearing at each other in the jungle and gossiping about who might fancy who. On the next night, they watch youngsters who are locked in a house together, in the hope a couple might decide to have sex or, second best, a row.

At times, it makes you think that, comparatively, it must have been riveting to live in a time when families gathered round a piano to sing hymns for their entertainment. At least there must have been some sense that life was real, back then.

Also, we were all British then, not an extra branch of the American dream. Now, we suffer The Simpsons night after night (and the American way of speaking) and Friends repeated almost nightly. Consequently, we are starved of anything that improves us or genuinely moves us.

The worst thing about so much of this type of television is that it crushes our imagination and limits our horizons. I see it all the time in my family: my brother has become so acclimatised to soaps and reality television that he no longer makes the effort to watch anything more stimulating or intellectually demanding. My sister is so addicted to Friends that life for her stops between 8pm and 9pm. For me, an early night with a book is usually the best move that can be made.

second problem
'Because' introduces cause and effect
implies why he does not like such shows: suggests criticism through use of 'gossiping', and our limited expectations

sarcasm
explains it is the unreality of reality shows that he dislikes

explains his dislike of American shows

cause and effect

how this affects us/why it upsets him

conclusion: sums up criticism

GOOD POINTS:

- The introduction introduces three aspects of TV which he dislikes.
- The dislikes are then explained in detail in separate paragraphs.
- The response concentrates on 'why' and 'how' rather than just 'what'.
- The language is entertaining – including imagery (food and eating) and sarcasm ('comparatively, it must have been riveting').
- Sentences, punctuation and paragraphs are assured, effective and varied.

CHECK YOURSELF QUESTION

Q Explain how you have dealt with difficult situations that have arisen in your life.

You might wish to write about:
- relationships with parents
- problems at school
- friends and their expectations
- any difficult situations you have encountered.

Answer is on pages 162–163.

Writing to describe

Writing to describe will be one of the options in Section B of Paper 2. The question will probably ask you to describe a person or place.

When writing to describe, you should concentrate on various high-quality features:

- a response which is effectively structured
- a striking introduction and conclusion
- the use of five senses, when describing places
- imagery.

It is essential that you produce description, not narrative, because this is not a story-telling option.

- It makes most sense to describe something or someone you really know about. Although it can be a temptation to describe a town in the United States or a mysterious individual from Siberia, unless you have precise knowledge of these subjects your response is unlikely to be convincing.

- However, if you do decide to describe a person you have invented, make sure his characteristics are based on people you do know well, so that he comes across as a real person.

- If you are describing a place, it is almost always best to describe a place where you have lived, or one you have visited.

An effective structure

- Because a description may involve many different aspects, it is particularly important that your ideas are collected into sections and linked effectively. Candidates who are tempted to begin writing without having planned carefully, run a serious risk of producing a response which lacks direction and offers only random, unstructured ideas.

- This is a detailed plan for a response to the question:

Describe a beach in August.

It should not be a story, but a detailed picture of what the beach is like.

PLAN
Intro: the atmosphere on the beach
  sounds, colours, sights, weather, people and games
Para 2: families
  dads red, mothers looking after babies and youngsters: wind breaks and deck chairs
Para 3: children
  on sands, in sea, digging and games, ice cream and sunburn
Para 4: sea
  sandy grey waves, seaweed, inflatables
Para 5: entertainments
  donkeys, volleyball, cricket, football, watching the girls/boys
Conclusion: view from the pier
  congested... tide coming in; movements, people drifting to steps and home

GOOD POINTS: ✓

- The response is clearly divided into sections.
- Although there is no narrative, a general structure is apparent: from arriving to leaving.

The introduction

- A vivid opening will immediately attract the attention of the examiner. There are various approaches which can achieve that effect. A C grade candidate is likely to produce an accurate but predictable first paragraph describing the beach:

> When I arrived at the beach, it was busy and exciting. Families in bright T-shirts were packed together, music blared and children were screaming. The sun beat down and the waves lapped against the shore.

- This is descriptive, but an A* candidate is likely to be less obvious and may choose to begin by concentrating on:

  - one family or individual, then broadening out the description
  - one particular area of the beach, which seems representative
  - one significant incident on the beach
  - personal reflections, on arrival at the beach
  or
  - quotation, to bring it all into immediate focus.

> 'Tommy! Tommy! You stop that right now! She's got sand in her eyes... I told you, didn't I? You wait till I get hold of you!' The beach was a heaving mass of families determined to enjoy themselves and banish the problems that plague them throughout the rest of the year...and failing. Everywhere across the drying sand, children laughed and cried, and parents rubbed on sun screens and screamed at errant sons and daughters. I had arrived on the hottest day of the year, and it seemed that people's tempers and tantrums matched the temperature.

quotation to capture sounds/atmosphere

immediate vision of packed beach

imaginative punctuation

focus on sounds, sights and behaviour

weather and tone set for rest of response

GOOD POINTS:

- The speech at the beginning captures the attention and presents the sort of voice we all recognise.
- The general atmosphere of the beach and the day is instantly established.
- Sounds and sights are both included.
- Sentence constructions are varied.

⚡ A* EXTRA

▸ An inventive opening is always the best. Speech grabs the reader's attention, as do introductory statements that are unusual or unexpected:
  - It is amazing how many people are prepared to sit around in their underwear on a British beach, when they would never dream of stripping off in their own home...
  - How did a man with a big red nose, swinging a string of sausages, who abuses his wife and child, ever come to win the affections of the beach-loving British public? Still, how we love Mr Punch...
  - Sand. Sea. Sun. Crowds. A strange paradise on earth: but a paradise, nevertheless...

◎ Including all five senses and imagery

- Good descriptive writing which deals with a place is likely to incorporate all five senses: sight, sound, taste, touch and smell. These do not need to be used equally, but if they are blended they will produce a more distinct impression.

- Imagery is another essential element. Similes and metaphors can capture what is happening in an original phrase, and illuminate a scene or the description of an individual.

The C grade response continues with an emphasis on sight and sound:

> Across the sands, there are windbreaks, in a variety of bright colours. In front of them are families, trying to find some privacy. Fathers are sitting or lying, reading the Daily Mirror or sleeping with it over their heads, turning red. Mothers are trying to control their children. Babies are rolling around on their backs and eating sand and older brothers and sisters are all begging for ice creams and drinks.

The A* response offers more variety, including all five senses and imagery:

sight
smells

sight

touch

> The windbreaks and T-shirts were bright, but everything else was just as loud. The air was rich with the smell of sun-tan cream and fried onions from hot-dog stalls, and lips tasted of sea salt and sand. All along the beach, fathers were ripening like red apples. They sat uncomfortably in deck chairs, reading their tabloids with sweat trickling down their necks or lay on towels, huge bellies rising like sand mounds from the waists of rolled-up trousers. Mothers, meanwhile, endeavoured to keep the children in check: shouting at boys and girls alike, who moaned back, 'It wasn't me, you always pick on me...' Babies looked hot and uncomfortable; the rough sand was scrubbing their sore arms and faces raw.

metaphor
taste

similes

sounds

GOOD POINTS:

- The senses heighten the seaside experience.
- Similes and metaphor are used to help the reader picture the fathers and imagine the atmosphere.
- Sentence control is impressive. Punctuation includes a colon, semi-colon, quotation marks and commas used helpfully.

◎ Conclusions

- Effective conclusions not only round off the response, but usually link clearly with the introduction. In this case, logic suggests the conclusion might well capture the final details as the writer leaves, since the introduction dealt with the arrival. Because this is the seaside, there is also the opportunity to offer new description, because the tide will have turned, the day will have moved on, and different things will be happening.

Look at this C grade response:

> Now, it is cooler in the late afternoon sun. The sand is mixed with litter and heaped in broken mounds. Families are heading home. They queue at the steps to leave the beach. The children are tired and quiet, and parents carry bags and towels. The tide is coming in again, and soon it will be cleaning all the mess away.

Now look at this A* grade conclusion:

> The sun is lower in the sky and the tide is creeping up the littered beach. Families retreat, then pack and go. Tommy and Sarah are tired and complain about carrying the ball and spade; father is burning bright, a deckchair in one hand, and his newspaper still in the other; and mother struggles with the push chair, laden with bags, over the sand. The heat has taken its toll, so now they are all drained, but calm. There is a queue by the steps from the beach and they join the shuffling masses, dutifully: a British end to a British day by the sea.

sense of time having moved on

leaving now

back to original family, identifiable from earlier

using such individuals makes it easier to relate to the experience

changed by the day

to end, a touch of humour about the British willingness to queue: to stress this was, throughout, a recognisably British beach and description

GOOD POINTS:

- The A* response is, once again, more vivid than the C grade one.
- This final paragraph links effectively with the details from the introduction: time has moved on and the same family is reviewed.

- The movement from the start of the day to going home is handled effectively, not just by the sinking of the sun, but with the details of what has changed (the people's energy levels, the increase in litter and sunburn).

- Language control is mature, and the vocabulary is effective ('creeping up the littered beach', 'laden with bags', 'join the shuffling masses, dutifully').

◉ Using a range of techniques

- Descriptions of people involve some slight differences – for example, there is less likelihood of the senses being used. It is possible you will include some description of background, as well as physical description.

The answer below blends a range of A* skills in response to the question:

Describe the person you most admire.

Some people choose sportsmen as their heroes; others choose men who have climbed mountains or won the Victoria Cross. However, the person I most admire is not famous or wealthy, lives just down the road from me and goes to the same school. His name is Jonathon and he is paralysed from the waist down. But he is an inspiration.

One thing he has taught me is that being unable to walk does not make you a suitable case for sympathy. And if anyone might welcome sympathy, you would have thought it might be him: he was tall; according to most girls, he was the Tom Cruise of Year 11; he captained the football team; he was Head Boy of the school and looked set for the brightest of futures... Then, just before his mock A levels, he went downhill on a sledge in the snow, backwards. And hit a tree.

When he woke up, he was in intensive care, still on his back, and was told he might never regain any movement below his neck.

He did, of course. Stoke Mandeville Hospital – and the most incredible will to get better and be mobile – saw him through. From the outset, he would not be patronised and did not want to be looked after for the rest of his life. He had too much living still to do.

Now, he motors round in his wheelchair like some sort of demented Michael Schumacher and does wheelies in the discos that make you want to cheer and weep – yes, he even has that effect on boys. He has also demonstrated that physical incapacity is no restriction on intellect, which is something we all know but sometimes find difficult to accept. Despite missing so many months, he looks set to pass all his exams with A grades, and should eventually get to a top university. He might not ever be able to row for Oxford, but he will make an excellent doctor, which is his ambition.

considered opening

an apparently 'everyday' style here, to introduce an 'ordinary' person: short sentences, unexceptional vocabulary

unexpected detail; short, dramatic final sentence

describes his attitude

physical description and description of abilities

description of how injured: complex sentence and startling ending

short, powerful paragraph emphasising severity of injury

description of qualities and attitude

humorous simile

describes effect he has on others

mature vocabulary

describes intellectual abilities

potential

One can only imagine the suffering he feels, when he is alone and unable to sleep, but it is not an emotion he reveals to the world. His arms are becoming stronger, he talks of completing a wheelchair marathon and convinces you that he will do it. Like Superman, who was similarly struck down, he will not accept his life has been ended by paraplegia. He tells you he will fly again.

Because of all this, Jonathon is greater than Wayne Rooney or Neil Armstrong or anyone else I have ever heard of. He is so normal, but also so incredibly different. He convinces you that he can do anything he sets his mind on – and makes you re-examine your own existence and values. If he can overcome such hurdles, there should be nothing to stop any of us.

GOOD POINTS:

- The response is well structured: introduction to his problems/what he was, and what happened to him/how he has recovered/positive views of future/what he means to the writer.
- There is description at every stage.
- When imagery is used, it creates an effect on the reader.
- The introduction and conclusion include memorable ideas.
- The writing is sensitive and touching ('yes, he even has that effect on boys…').

⚡ A* EXTRA

▸ When describing someone, rather than just writing subjectively and giving your own views it might sometimes be appropriate to:
- include a conversation with them – to highlight how they talk or think
- include an anecdote about them
- present someone else's view of them
- include a newspaper report about them and so on, to provide variety and originality.

❓ CHECK YOURSELF QUESTION

Q Describe a place where you spend much of your time.

You might like to choose:
- a park
- a swimming pool
- a gym
- a club

or anywhere else that is appropriate.

Answer is on pages 163–5.

Blending types of writing

Section B on both English papers will offer you a choice of four questions, from which you must select one. Three questions will require you to write in the styles we have dealt with in the previous sessions:

- argue, persuade, advise (Paper 1)
- inform, explain, describe (Paper 2).

However, the fourth question on each paper will require you to blend the types of writing you have learnt. So, for example:

- a question on Paper 1 might ask you to argue, persuade and advise
- a question on Paper 2 might require a response which informs and explains.

◎ Blending skills on Paper 1

- Any mixing of skills is possible. If you know how to deal with each type of writing, choosing the blended option may be a good idea, because you have the opportunity to exhibit a wide range of skills. Also, of course, the 'triplet' involves types of writing which are closely related.

For instance, if the question required it, you could:
- start with contradictory viewpoints (argument)
- go on to explain why one approach is preferable (persuasion)
- conclude by saying what should be done in the light of these ideas (advice).

- This title would fit into this pattern:

> Imagine you work as an agent for people who are regularly in the news.
>
> Write a letter to **advise** a celebrity how to avoid publicity they would not welcome. In your letter:
> • **argue** that it is possible to maintain some privacy, although not easy
> • **persuade** them of the benefits of this behaviour
> • **advise** them how to safeguard their privacy.

In this case, your response might well break into three neat sections:

1. The argument:
   Reports and photographers will follow you everywhere, so there can be no escape; celebrity stories help newspapers sell
   but:
   if you do not court publicity and do nothing the tabloids can expose, you can remain relatively private.

2. The persuasion:
   Avoiding bad publicity will lessen stresses with wife/within family; and will generate sponsorship deals/advertising/additional income; and will mean life can be balanced and more pleasant.

3. The advice:
   Never let down your guard or let anyone know your movements outside the immediate family; confirm a good public image by undertaking charity work, etc; aim to offend no one in the media, so then they will not seek vengeance.

Make sure you get my good side, darling.

Confirming a good public image…

> **GOOD POINTS:** ✔
> - The three types of writing are included.
> - The requirements of the question are all addressed.
> - By placing the advice at the end, there is logical progression:
>   – the two sides
>   – persuasion that one point of view should hold sway
>   – advice to make the situation come about.

■ Although the ways in which responses can be structured vary enormously, there should always be an internal logic to the development of your ideas. Regardless of the way the title is presented, if you are dealing with all three skills, the argument-persuasion-advice sequence is usually the most effective.

■ On some occasions, however, it might be more effective to integrate the types of writing more fully, for example when dealing with this title:

> Write a speech to be given to your year group, in which you **argue** that they could do more to make the school successful and **persuade** them to accept your views.

In this case, one approach could be:

1. Point of view that Year 11 is already very committed:
   - undertake a range of charity activities and sports events
   - work as prefects within the school
   - look set to achieve excellent GCSE results

2. Point of view that they could do more, and persuade them why they should:

   - Some Year 11s not involved in extra-curricular work at all: could improve school's profile in the community – e.g. clean-up campaigns locally, charity events, working with the Rotary Club - and help themselves, through Record of Achievement, etc.

   - Could offer more time to support weaker students lower down the school in academic work (e.g. for 30 minutes after school, or at breaks and lunchtimes) and help with their teams and clubs: personal satisfaction, working alongside the staff who have helped them, pleasure of seeing others improve.

   - Could be organising all those things the school would welcome but cannot currently undertake because of other calls on staff time: fund-raising through fun runs, sponsored events, etc. This involvement will look good on their CVs.

> **GOOD POINTS:**
> - The response involves argument and persuasion.
> - The side of the argument which is being outweighed comes first.
> - The counter arguments and persuasion are appropriately linked, so that each idea can be precisely developed and the persuasion can be made appropriate when the response is written.

◎Blending skills on Paper 2

■ The approach you need to adopt for Paper 2 is very similar. For example, the exam question might link 'inform' and 'explain', because they fit well together. A question might well ask you to write informatively about an event and explain why the event happened or the effect it had or why it was memorable.

■ Alternatively, you might be asked to describe a place that you have found frightening and explain your reactions. In this case, there would be two possible approaches:

1. Integrating the skills:
   - When we first approached Whitby Abbey: ruin on the hill overlooking the sea - how I felt (memories of Dracula – novel set here - etc).
   - Walking up the steps towards it – what it was like and what was around (ruined tower) - and effect of impending doom.
   - Investigating the ruins: through the church itself, the chambers, piles of stones, wind freezing on the cliff-top - sense of others who had walked there, inability to shake mind free of vampire legends.
   - Sea mist coming down, visibility reduced, clammy air, noises – terror, rushed back down to the town and the harbour.
   - Renewed visions and nightmares that night.

2. Using separate sections:
   - A detailed description of the Abbey as we walked around.
   - Reactions, and why - unease: psychological factors, memories of Dracula novel, relative quietness around ruins in mid-winter, effect of misty weather – need to escape and how I felt afterwards.

GOOD POINTS:

- Both of these responses describe and explain.
- The first describes and explains the feelings at each stage: it manages to focus on description rather than narrative, even though the description moves through different phases.
- The second makes a clear and logical division: it describes the abbey, then works through the range of reactions, explaining why they occurred.

■ It is possible that the question might ask you to inform, explain and describe. For example:

> Write a section of a leaflet for tourists, **describing** a building you feel merits a visit. Give **information** about the building and **explain** why it deserves to be visited.

IMPORTANT!

When dealing with a question of this kind, remember that this is an English exam and you will receive no marks for artwork. Some candidates waste time on presentational devices instead of producing a high quality piece of writing. If you wish to show an awareness of the genre, give a quick impression of how it might be set out, but in 45 minutes you do not have the time to include crafted designs.

It is usually better to avoid writing in columns, even if a particular form of writing – in this case, a leaflet – might usually be produced in that form. Once a page is divided into columns, candidates almost always write in much shorter, tabloid-style paragraphs, and do not exhibit the range of skills expected for a top grade.

⚡ A* EXTRA

▸ A way of adding to this simple organisation is to include some organisational devices which might well appear in a leaflet and which would be appropriate for this particular task. Sub-headings could be used to support the text: *An Unforgettable Location, A Window on History, An Attraction that Caters for Everyone.*

Plan for Tourist leaflet: Tower of London

1. Description: beside Thames/imposing structure/ different sections/high walls/beefeaters/ravens/ crown jewels

2. Information: built 1078/100 ft high walls up to 5 metres thick/several monarchs died there/death of Princes in the Tower/ghost of Anne Boleyn/became a museum in 1603

3. Explanation: therefore, much of interest at the Tower for all age groups – children love the beefeaters and jewels, grown-ups can learn lots of English history, really old can just sit and admire the wonderful views.

GOOD POINTS:

- All three types of writing are addressed.
- In following the demands of the question, there is a logical sequence:
  – what it looks like: first impressions and description
  – its history: i.e. giving information beyond the obvious
  – an explanation of why, therefore, it is worth a visit.

? CHECK YOURSELF QUESTION

Q Produce a detailed outline, like those above, to show how you would tackle this title:

'Write an article for a teenage magazine in which you attempt to **persuade** the readers to adopt a healthier lifestyle.

In your article:
- **argue** that an improved lifestyle is achievable although it may take time
- **persuade** the readers that it is worth aiming for
- **advise** readers about what they need to do.'

Answer is on page 165.

EXAM PRACTICE

Paper 1

Time: 1 hour 45 minutes

Answer **all questions in Section A and one question from Section B.**

Spend approximately 60 minutes on Section A and 45 minutes on Section B.

Section A

Reading: Non-fiction and Media Texts

Youngsters want their mums to be like Marge from *The Times*

Mother of truant sent back to prison from *Guardian Unlimited* website

1 **Read the newspaper article**, *Youngsters want their mums to be like Marge* (page 122).

   a) How are facts and opinions used to create an impression of Marge?

   (6 marks)

   b) What are the effects of the layout and presentational devices?

   (5 marks)

   Read the website report, *Mother of truant sent back to prison* (page 124)

   c) According to the article:
   i) what is being done to reduce truancy?
   ii) is the action effective?

   (8 marks)

Compare the two texts.

   d) Both texts deal with parenting. Which is the more interesting?

   Compare them by writing about:

   • use of language

   • purpose and audience.

   (8 marks)

Mark schemes and sample answers are on pages 128–135.

Section B

Writing: to argue, persuade, advise

EITHER

2 Parents can be held responsible for their children in various ways. They can even be held responsible if their children truant from school.

   Write an article for a national newspaper in which you **argue** that parents **should or should not** be held responsible for the actions of their children.

   (27 marks)

OR

3 Increasingly, students are continuing to study after taking GCSEs.

   Write the text of a speech to be delivered at a careers convention for schools, to **persuade** the students of the benefits of gaining educational qualifications.

   (27 marks)

OR

4 Many people believe that politicians have never been held in such low esteem.

   Write a letter to a leading politician, to offer **advice** on how to create a good impression with the public.

   (27 marks)

OR

5 We are all affected by the actions of others, and have people we admire.

   Write an article for your school magazine, in which you:

   • **argue** in favour of good role models

   • seek to **persuade** the readers to accept your own suggestions.

   (27 marks)

Mark schemes and sample answers are on pages 136–138.

Youngsters want their mums to be like Marge

20TH CENTURY FOX

By Ruth Gledhill
Religion Correspondent

AT OVER 6ft tall with her blue beehive hair, strapless green dresses and politically incorrect cartoon lifestyle, Marge Simpson might not appear the obvious role model.

But a survey by the Mothers' Union has shown that the nation's young people idealise the woman — who just manages to hold the Simpson family together — as the best mother in public life, better even than Cherie Blair. Marge Simpson's down-to-earth approach and advice, such as telling her three children to "listen to your heart, and not the voices in your head", is widely admired.

Young people would love their own mothers to be similarly open and frank, particularly about the facts of life.

In response to the question, "What one thing do you wish your mother had told you?", the most common response was that they wished they had been told more about sex.

In spite of their apparently chaotic lifestyle, the Simpson parents are becoming role models across society. At a conference on fatherhood four years ago, Homer, Marge's fat, bald husband who pawned the television set so that he could pay to put his family through group therapy, was held up as a father to be admired. Even Rowan Williams, the Archbishop of Canter-

MARGE SIMPSON

■ Aged 34 and stands at eight feet, hair included.

■ She has three children including a baby.

■ She has been known to pull a jar of cash, a cat, a chicken and a cheque to cover damages to her husband's car from her hair.

■ Her husband works in a nuclear power plant.

■ Marge has flirted briefly with various careers from police officer to anti-violence activist.

■ She was nearly seduced into a life of crime by a neighbour.

■ She met Homer when in detention for burning her bra.

■ Other characters include an incompetent lawyer.

Sayings include: "I don't want you wearing rings. It looks cheap. But three."

"Well, anyone who beats you up for wearing a shirt isn't your friend."

CHERIE BLAIR

■ Aged 49

■ She has four children including a toddler.

■ She once apologised for misleading the public about her receiving financial advice on two buy-to-let flats from fraudster Peter Foster.

■ She is a lawyer and a champion of the oppressed and those who face discrimination in society.

■ Her husband runs the country.

■ Was fined for fare-dodging.

■ She met Tony when they both studied law.

■ Characters include a lifestyle guru.

■ Sayings include: "As long as young people feel they have got no hope but to blow themselves up you are never going to make progress."

Once said that being a mum "was the most important job of all".

bury and a patron of the Mothers' Union, said *The Simpsons* is one of his favourite television programmes.

More than 400 people were questioned for the survey by the Mothers' Union, an Anglican charity with three million members worldwide dedicated to promoting marriage and family life.

Asked which mother in the public spotlight they considered to be a good role model for other mothers, 23.2 per cent named Marge Simpson. Next most popular were Lorraine Kelly, the television presenter, with 18.8 per cent of the vote, and Mrs Blair on 15.2 per cent. Victoria Beckham polled 12.7 per cent, ahead

of Sharon Osbourne, with 12 per cent. The least popular mother was Elizabeth Hurley, backed by just 5 per cent.

Which women are your role models?

Send your e-mails to **debate@thetimes.co.uk**

With links to the very best of
education resources and information

TeacherNet: what you need, when you need it

Sign in | Register

Go to: [Guardian Unlimited home ◆] [Go]

EducationGuardian.co.uk **Schools special reports**

Home | Higher | Schools news | FE news | TEFL news | Education weekly | Jobs | Talk | Help
| Links | Interactive guides | Special reports | Archive search | Learn.co.uk | Clearing |

Truancy

Mother of truant sent back to prison

First parent to be jailed is inside again after daughter skips school

Lucy Ward, education correspondent
Wednesday March 24, 2004
The Guardian

A mother who became the first parent in Britain to be jailed for letting her children play truant was yesterday sent to prison again for the same offence after her youngest daughter repeatedly skipped school.

Patricia Amos, from Banbury, Oxfordshire, was sentenced by Bicester magistrates to 28 days' imprisonment after failing to ensure her 14-year-old daughter, Jacqueline, attended lessons regularly. She had denied the charge, saying she had made "every effort" to get her daughter to go to school.

Amos was jailed for 60 days in May 2002 because Jacqueline and her older sister, Emma, persistently played truant from Banbury school. She was released on appeal after 28 days and vowed to make her daughters attend lessons, but after initial improvement - including a school prize for Emma - Jacqueline's attendance slipped again to 61% last autumn.

Amos, 45, whose solicitor yesterday told the court she believed she had been made a scapegoat for all parents whose children truanted, was convicted under toughened legislation introduced under a government crackdown on truancy.

A DfES spokeswoman declined to comment on Amos's case, but said: "There is a significant package of investment and measures to give parents every support, understanding and assistance to tackle the underlying causes of truancy.

Search this site
[   ] [Search]

Find a job
[   ] [Go]
Detailed search

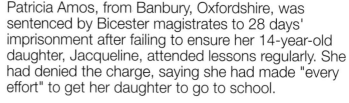

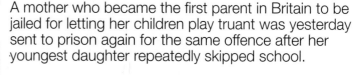

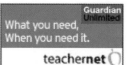

What you need,
When you need it.

teachernet

"However, where parents are not unable, but simply unwilling, to fulfil their responsibilities, legal sanctions through prosecution or penalty notices must apply."

Oxfordshire county council rejected suggestions it could have done more to work with Amos, a former heroin user, to improve Jacqueline's attendance, insisting she had been offered high levels of support but had ultimately refused to accept it.

A spokesman said: "A parent's refusal to engage meaningfully with the support offered is a factor in determining whether or not to prosecute.

"It should be noted that the offence in this case relates not simply to having failed to secure a pupil's attendance but of having condoned the absence." The council's support measures had prevented the vast majority of similar truancy cases ever reaching court, he added.

Around 7,500 parents are prosecuted each year, according to the DfES, for failing to ensure their child's regular attendance at school, with a guilty verdict in 80% of cases and most others withdrawn when a parent agrees to work with education welfare services.

However, the government also faced criticism for its "cruel" use of prison for parents. Rob Allen, the director of Rethinking Crime and Punishment, which researches alternatives to prison, said: "Sending the parents of truants to prison is both cruel and ineffective. While there is no doubting the importance of a good education it is hard to see how imprisoning the parent of a truant and removing them from their family helps anyone."

EducationGuardian.co.uk © Guardian Newspapers Limited 2004

Time: 1 hour 30 minutes

Answer **one question from Section A and one question from Section B.**

Spend approximately 45 minutes on each Section.

You are allowed to refer to a copy of the Anthology in the examination.

Section A

Reading: Poems from Different Cultures and Traditions

1 Compare the way of life presented in *Two Scavengers in a Truck, Two Beautiful People in a Mercedes* with that presented in any other poem of your choice from 'Poems from Different Cultures and Traditions'.

Write about:

• what we learn of the people

• the kind of society in which they live

• how language is used by the poets.

(27 marks)

OR

2 In some of the poems from 'Poems from Different Cultures and Traditions', individuals are worried about their identities: who they are or who they seem to be.

Compare *from Search For My Tongue* with any other poem of your choice, explaining:

• the problems revealed in the poems

• how the poets feel about the situation

• how language and structure are used.

(27 marks)

Mark schemes and sample answers are on pages 141–145.

Section B

EITHER

3 Write a letter to the Prime Minister.

Inform him about what life is like for teenagers today, what needs to be improved and how he can help.

(27 marks)

OR

4 **Explain** what you have enjoyed most about your years in school.

(27 marks)

OR

5 We usually know most about those closest to us.

Write a **description** of a member of your family.

(27 marks)

OR

6 Write an article for a magazine that is sold abroad, **informing** the readers about how most Britons spend their leisure time, and **explaining** why.

(27 marks)

Mark schemes and sample answers are on pages 136–140.

Answers and Mark Schemes

The mark schemes included here are similar to those used by examiners. The grids all include descriptors alongside grades. Throughout, the examiners operate a **'best fit' system**, weighing up the strengths and weaknesses of responses so they can award the most correct 'all-round' mark or grade.

If a response demonstrates all the skills required for a 'C' but also touches into the 'B' category, the mark awarded will be at the bottom of the 'B' band. If a response fulfils most of the 'C' descriptors but not all, it is likely to be awarded a 'mid C', rather than a 'top C'.

Use the mark schemes to award your responses the best fit grade. **Extracts from student responses** – with annotations highlighting their strengths and weaknesses – are also included to help you understand what the descriptors in the mark scheme mean in practice.

MARK SCHEME: PAPER 1 SECTION A

In this section, the **Skills Descriptors** are the most important element, and you need to use these to determine the correct mark/grade. The **Content Descriptors** are included to give some examples of what a response might include. If other material is used, that is fine, as long as the skills are in evidence. Obviously, a higher grade is merited if the content is dealt with more thoroughly with fuller analysis.

Simple comments limit an answer to the lower grades ('This shows that she is kind'); more **developed ideas** move it towards the middle of the grade range ('We know that she is kind, because when she... her actions help us understand that...'); and **thorough analysis** moves it to the top of the range ('When we examine her words and actions, we realise that she is kind. For example... This reveals her warm personality, as she is like.... Not only that, she also says... which makes us think that... Furthermore...')

QI a) How are facts and opinions used to create an impression of Marge?

Mark/Grade		Skills Descriptors	Content Descriptors
0	U	• nothing written	Response is likely to focus on:
I	G/F	• mostly paraphrase of texts • little evidence of understanding use of fact and opinion	**Facts:** • initial description • bulleted points
2–3	E/D	• attempts to deal with facts and opinions • identifies and comments on facts and opinions	• (possibly, contrast with facts presented for Mrs Blair)
4–5	C/B	• clear understanding of how facts and opinions used • structured and detailed analysis	• voting percentage **Opinions:** presented by correspondent, such as:
6	A/A*	• evaluates use of facts and opinions (says how successfully they are used) • thorough analysis, which is sophisticated and convincing	• 'politically incorrect lifestyle' • 'idealise' • 'down-to-earth approach' • 'Young people would love their own mothers to be similarly...' • 'becoming role models across society'

Sample answer: C grade

Generally, the facts and opinions present Marge in a positive way.

The facts describe her strange looks, such as her 'blue beehive hair', and one of the bullets talks about the things she can pull from her hair. However, the bullets generally are facts telling us about her life, and they are not all showing her strangeness. We are told about when she met Homer and what careers she has tried: 'from police officer to anti-violence activist'. Like many other women, she has three children, and she is popular, because she got 23.2% of the vote.

We are presented with Marge's own opinions, such as 'Well, anyone who beats you up for wearing a shirt isn't your friend'. This is to show us why people like her, because of her good sense. The writer's opinions also seem to make her appear a kind of heroine. We are told, 'Young people would love their own mothers to be similarly open and frank.' This opinion shows her in a good light again.

Overall, the facts and opinions give a fair picture of the Marge we all know from television. She looks silly but tries to be a good mother.

structured: balanced opening

section on facts: details used throughout

clear on how facts used

facts mentioned, but without analysis

section on opinions

appropriate quotation again

shows use of opinion though many opinions omitted

sensible summative comment

Examiner's comments
- This response is clear on how the facts and opinions are used, has structure (introduction/facts/opinions/conclusion) and relevant detail.
- However, the analysis needed to be more thorough – note, for example, that two facts are mentioned without specific comment – and only two opinions are mentioned, with appropriate but limited comments. This lack of analysis is mirrored in the conclusion: 'She looks silly but tries to be a good mother'.
- A higher grade response would have included more sophisticated analysis, which showed more clearly the writer's point of view, and might have analysed the impression of Marge in relation to the image of Cherie Blair, deciding whether the writer really approved of the survey's results.

Q1 b) What are the effects of the layout and presentational devices?

Mark/Grade		Skills Descriptors	Content Descriptors
0	U	• nothing written	Responses are likely to examine:
I	G/F	• mostly describes the texts • little evidence of understanding layout and presentation	• pictures, including colour; effect of these images of Marge and Mrs Blair
2–3	E/D	• attempts to engage with task • selects relevant features • attempts to make appropriate comments	• bulleted points beside pictures, for comparison • headline, including font and positioning; possibly columns
4–5	C/B	• clear understanding of effects of layout and presentational devices • structured and detailed analysis • uses appropriate media language	• shaded box to conclude • (missing bullet in Marge list)
6	A/A*	• evaluates use of layout and presentational devices • thorough analysis • effective use of media language	

Sample answer: A* grade

The newspaper article is likely to attract the reader's interest because of the pictures. The colourful picture of Marge is placed centrally, which is effective because it catches the reader's eye; then the headline is aligned to the left, so the reader moves to that later.

evaluates layout (says why it is effective)

The picture of Marge shows her vivid (and weird) sense of fashion, which most readers will recognise immediately – and those who do not will be attracted anyway, since high blue hair is not at all normal. She is being hailed as the ideal mother, so it is appropriate that she seems calm and is surrounded by pink, to stress her femininity. In contrast, and appropriately, the subliminal impression of Mrs Blair is that she looks 'defeated'. She has dark leather clothes, seems to be rushed and looks in pain. We are supposed to conclude it is no wonder that Marge came out on top.

understands the effect

thorough analysis

again, evaluates: effect of presentation

The headline is in large bold type. The intention is probably to make the reader wonder whether it is surprising that 'Youngsters want their mums to be like Marge' considering Marge's appearance, but then the reader would conclude that she does look, somehow, more comforting than Mrs Blair. In other words, the headline works effectively with the pictures.

media language used effectively throughout

As well as having a cartoon image of the winner, the article uses another technique to give facts about her and about Mrs Blair: details are bulleted, so the two

analyses how presentational elements combine

women can be quickly and easily compared. This suggests that the newspaper thinks the article may attract younger readers - because of the subject matter and presentation - and so uses a style with which they are familiar to set out the information.

analysing effect of presentation

The only other significant presentational feature is the text box to conclude. Sensibly, it is shaded, to attract attention, since the writer is hoping readers will e-mail details of their own role models - perhaps so that there can be another article about women who the writer feels are more suitable as role models for the young.

able to offer evaluation and explanation of why feature has been included

Examiner's comments

- The candidate indicates that she knows why the layout and devices have been used and comments on their effectiveness.
- The analysis is thorough, including all the significant elements; and media language is always used effectively ('aligned', 'subliminal', 'font', 'headline', 'bulleted', 'text box').

Q1 c) According to the article:

   i)   what is being done to reduce truancy?

   ii) is the action effective?

Mark/Grade		Skills Descriptors	Content Descriptors
0	U	• nothing written	Responses are likely to examine:
1–2	G/F	• mostly paraphrases the text • little evidence of understanding the actions or effects	• toughened legislation • jailing of parents • support for parents
3–4	E/D	• attempts to engage with task • selects relevant features • attempts to make appropriate comments	• Patricia Amos released then imprisoned again • parents have to agree to work with authorities
5–6	C/B	• clear understanding of effects of actions and effects • begins to analyse • a competent response	• most cases not taken to court • but 7,500 prosecuted each year • 80% guilty; others agree to work with welfare services
7–8	A/A*	• evaluates actions and effects • thorough analysis • sophisticated and convincing	• some feel imprisonment and splitting families is not the answer

EXAM PRACTICE

Sample answer: C grade

Action is being taken against parents of truants but it does not always work.

There are new laws now and parents are going to prison if their children fail to attend school. According to the article, lots of parents seem to improve when they have to work with education welfare services, and their children must attend school more regularly, but this was not the case with Patricia Amos. She has had to be sent back to prison, because her daughter only attended school for 61% last autumn. Not only that, 7,500 other parents are prosecuted each year and 80% of them are found guilty. Rob Allen, who is in charge of Rethinking Crime and Punishment, believes something else needs to be done, because it is a bad thing to split up families and take parents away from their children.

clear overview

understanding of authorities' methods: notes some success

recognises apparent failures

conclusion focuses on need for a different approach

Examiner's comments

- The response shows clear understanding of the text, noting both the measures being taken against the parents and how effective they seem to be. The initial overview is supported in the main body of the response. First, there are the signs of improvement; then the response moves to illustration of why the system is not perfect. The case of Patricia Amos is highlighted, along with relevant statistics. Finally, Rob Allen's views are used to suggest that the government's approach cannot be good for either the parents or the children. The examination of both sides shows the beginning of analysis.

- To gain a higher grade, the candidate would have to examine the text in more precise detail: for example, the emotive language used by Amos' solicitor ('scapegoat', 'crackdown') as opposed to the language used by the DfES spokeswoman ('investment', 'support, understanding and assistance'). Vocabulary like this sums up contrasting views of the strategy. The candidate also failed to mention the spokesman's opinion that 'meaningful engagement' with support is all that is needed to avoid further action. Because the candidate seems to lean towards the view that the strategy is often failing, other significant quotations are also omitted, such as: "The council's support measures had prevented the vast majority of similar cases ever reaching court, he added."

- A thorough analysis might also have examined the structure of the article: how it begins with the 'hard news' story, of Patricia Amos being sent to jail; but ends with a judgement by a critic, saying that such action is 'cruel and ineffective'. The response might then have decided whether the article is an objective review, or whether the writer tried to influence the reader to support a particular side of the argument.

Q1 d) Both texts deal with parenting. Which is the more interesting?

Compare them by writing about:
• use of language
• purpose and audience.

Mark/Grade		Skills Descriptors	Content Descriptors
0	U	• nothing written	Possible content:
1–2	G/F	• mostly paraphrases the text • little evidence of understanding how language used or of purpose and audience	*Youngsters want their mums to be like Marge* **Language:** • mostly complex sentences
3–4	E/D	• attempts to engage with task • selects relevant language features • generalises on purpose and audience • attempts to make appropriate comments and to compare	• Marge 'flirted', 'seduced'; Homer 'fat, bald', 'pawned' • but also positives on Marge: 'admired', 'would love' and Homer 'admired' • use of quotations/statistics
5–6	C/B	• clear understanding of how language used • purpose and audience clear • begins to analyse • clear comparison of success	**Purpose and audience:** • inform/entertain: 'soft news' • to encourage people to think about the survey's findings (two sides of the Simpsons presented)
7–8	A/A*	• evaluates use of language • thorough analysis, of language and purpose and audience • sophisticated and convincing comparison throughout	• broadsheet audience: though layout also might attract younger readers *Mother of truant sent back to prison* **Language:** • complex sentences again • legal language: 'offence', 'sentenced', 'imprisonment' etc • facts/figures significant • spokeswoman uses sort of abstractions often favoured by politicians: 'significant package', 'investment and measures', 'support, understanding and assistance' etc • 'criticism' and 'cruel' stand out at the end **Purpose and audience:** • inform/present arguments for and against government measures • for intelligent readership (sentences and vocabulary), perhaps with an interest in families/society/justice

Sample answer: A* grade

The use of language is not dissimilar in the two texts, because both are aimed at an intelligent readership. They have slightly different purposes, and are aimed at slightly different audiences but they can both be considered interesting in their own ways.

deals with question in general terms to begin: language, interest level and purpose and audience

From the first sentence, which is complex and constitutes a complete paragraph, the article on 'Marge' is clearly aimed at an educated broadsheet audience. Significantly, too, the voting figures at the end are placed in sentences, rather than being tabulated, which assumes the readers do not need them simplifying.

language linked to audience

Impressions are created subtly, so that our interest is stirred. Marge might have won the vote, but we are told she 'flirted' and was 'seduced': both terms imply criticism and have connotations of sexual infidelity. Her husband, meanwhile, is described in unflattering terms ('fat, bald') and, although for a good cause, he 'pawned' the television. Taken together, this language creates a poor impression of the Simpsons. The way the writer opens with a description of 'beehive hair' and 'strapless green dresses' also suggests that this role model is being patronised, because it does not present a flattering image. There is some positive language used (she is 'admired', and 'open and frank'), but the memorable phrases are the critical ones, like 'chaotic lifestyle'.

analyses language

well-chosen quotations

further analysis

In contrast, Cherie Blair is 'a champion of the oppressed'. The metaphor is successful in promoting a heroic image, and she might also appeal to the readers because she is made to seem very British – 'being a mum "was the most important job of all"'. 'Mum' is a peculiarly British term.

analyses and evaluates effect of language

The second text has a different purpose. Rather than dealing with playful comparisons between a national figure and a yellow cartoon character, the website article news report sets out simply to show the readers what has happened to Patricia Amos, and why; and to present two sides of an argument about the best ways to limit truancy and deal with failing parents.

sophisticated comparison of purpose and audience

clarifies purposes within the paragraph

Unlike the first writer, this one is no doubt assuming the target audience will be surfing for news and analysis and possibly even researching this subject.

further comparison: audience

As if to show she knows her subject well, she uses facts ('Amos was jailed for 60 days in May 2002'; 'Around 7,500 parents are prosecuted each year') and also opinions 'There is a significant package of investment and measures...'). She also balances the philosophy of the government, which is couched in abstract generalities ('legal sanctions through prosecution or penalty notices must apply') with the more abrasive vocabulary of those opposed to it. Amos' solicitor, for example, describes her as a 'scapegoat' and the Biblical metaphor makes her appear to be suffering for the sins of society in general. Rob Allen, meanwhile, uses words like 'cruel' to criticise the government, and leaves us with an emotive vision of families torn apart: 'it is hard to see how imprisoning the parent of a truant and removing them from their family helps anyone.'

The readers, therefore, are left to decide which side they should take. Presumably, they are interested by the dilemma itself and by the way it has been presented.

In that each text is effectively asking the reader to make a choice, they are similar. Also, they both use complex language. However, since their purposes are different, it is impossible to say which is more interesting. The simple sentences in the lists - along with the pictures - are likely to attract younger people to the 'Marge' article, and the subtlety of the implications might appeal to older readers. Meanwhile, the presentation of a complex real life issue will make the webpage a valuable source of news and information for surfers.

deals with aspects of the language

evaluates effect of language

summarising features of interest

sophisticated comparison to conclude

Examiner's comments

- This is a very lengthy and detailed comparison which evaluates how language is used and analyses it, alongside purpose and audience, whilst including evaluation of the effects achieved. The stem of the question is handled, as well as the bullet points.
- It is always convincing, despite adopting one particular interpretation of the news article (that Cherie Blair is favoured by the writer over Marge Simpson); and makes some sophisticated points. It is as good as could be expected of a sixteen-year-old.

Overall Grade for Paper 1, Section A

Total marks	Grade
0	U
1-3	G
4-6	F
7-10	E
11-13	D
14-18	C
19-21	B
22-24	A
25-27	A*

MARK SCHEME: PAPER 1 SECTION B AND PAPER 2 SECTION B

Examiners will award two separate marks for your Section B responses: one will be for **Communication and organisation** – worth two-thirds of your total mark for this section - and the other for **Sentences, punctuation and spelling** – worth one-third of your marks for this section.

Whichever writing task you have chosen to complete, use this grid to work out how well you have done.

Sample extracts from students' answers have been included for Paper 1 Questions 2 and 5 and Paper 2 Questions 5 and 6.

Grade	Communication and organisation	Sentences, punctuation and spelling
U	• some meaning • simple ideas	• some sentences • punctuation random • some very simple words spelt correctly
G	• some sense of purpose and audience • ideas sequenced simply	• sentences used • simple punctuation used: some full stops • generally accurate spelling of simple words
F	• clearer sense of purpose and audience • tries to link ideas • random paragraphs • some words chosen because they suit the task	
E	• clear awareness of purpose and audience • beginning to use the correct vocabulary • paragraphs used more accurately • attempts vocabulary for effect, such as discourse markers, emotive language and rhetoric	• secure sentences, probably using discourse markers • capitals and full stops used accurately and a range of punctuation • commonly used words spelt correctly, and some more complex words
D	• generally suitable for purpose and audience • correct vocabulary most of time and interests the reader • paragraphs organise the response, but tend to be the same length and are not well linked • uses some vocabulary for effect	
C	• purpose and audience clear • sustains the reader's interest, possibly using anecdotes, examples, humour, rhetoric • paragraphs well linked • vocabulary used for effect	• sentences for effect, including sentences with different constructions and of different length • punctuation varied and generally accurate, using commas accurately, questions marks etc. • spelling mostly correct, including more complex words
B	• form, content and style appropriate for purpose and audience • detailed content, using effective features to influence the reader's reactions • well structured, with paragraphs developing the meaning • wide vocabulary	

A	• form, content and style consistently appropriate for purpose and audience • subtlety, to influence the reader • fluent response, with ideas presented in an original way • mature, advanced vocabulary	• full range of appropriate sentence structures, possibly including repetition for effect, contrasts, similar phrases for a purpose etc. • a high level of technical accuracy in punctuation, including colons and semi-colons where appropriate
A*	• form, content and style assuredly matched to purpose and audience throughout • advanced skills such as irony and satire when appropriate • an impressive and thoroughly effective structure • vocabulary which impresses and delights the reader	• a high level of technical accuracy in spelling

The standard expected of responses at 'C' and 'A*' level are illustrated in these annotated extracts from student responses.

PAPER 1 SECTION B

Q2 Parents can be held responsible for their children in various ways.

They can even be held responsible if their children truant from school.

Write an article for a national newspaper in which you **argue** that parents **should or should not** be held responsible for the actions of their children.

Extract from a C grade response

It is crazy that parents should be punished if their sons or daughters truant from school. After all, when someone becomes a teenager, they know what they want to do – and they do it, whatever their parents say.

Imagine, for example, how a parent might have to struggle if a sixteen year old refuses to go to school. What is the mother supposed to do? Does she send her sixteen year old son to his room? Does she stop his sweety money? Of course she can't. It's madness to expect her to be able to do anything.

Mind you, some people say that if children are brought up properly, there won't be a problem and it's down to the parents from the start. But it's not as simple as that. You can bring your kids up really well, but if they make some bad friends they are led astray easily, like when they are out on the streets. They might go off the rails then and that has nothing to do with the parents...

Annotations:
- strong sense of purpose
- complex sentence
- links paragraphs and sustains interest: example used and rhetorical questions
- accurate punctuation
- vocabulary for effect
- short, effective sentence
- linked paragraphs again opposing argument
- sentences of different construction and length
- purpose still clear

Examiner's comments

- This response displays most of the features of a C grade response. There is more than one point of view; it sustains our interest, using, for example, the brief example and rhetorical questions; the paragraphs are well linked and 'sweety' is used for effect. The sentences are of different lengths, punctuation is varied and accurate and spelling is correct, though there are not really any complex words.
- However, although there is a sense of purpose, this reads more like a speech than an article for a newspaper audience. From the opening ('It is crazy'), it seems powerful but a little informal ('Mind you...', 'kids').

- To achieve a higher grade, the response would need to be more suited to purpose and audience, in terms of the language used; the vocabulary would need to be more advanced ('allowance' might, for example, have been substituted for 'money'); and there would need to be more subtlety in the way the argument is presented.
- The style would need to be more mature – and less like a well-meaning rant – with ideas presented more originally. Perhaps the example of the teenager could have been developed into an anecdote, for example. The touch of sarcasm ('sweety money') might have been supplemented with irony elsewhere. The examiner would also have been impressed if a colon and semi-colons had been included.

Q5 We are all affected by the actions of others, and have people we admire.
Write an article for your school magazine, in which you:
- **argue** in favour of good role models
- seek to **persuade** the readers to accept your own suggestions.

Extract from an A* grade response

...After all, even though these sickeningly over-paid footballers are rich and these silky-thighed divas have the world at their feet (which are beautifully pedicured, naturally), it does not mean they make good role models. We should admire and seek to emulate those who have bravery or intelligence; or those who help others needing support and comfort.

And there are good role models all around us. You do not have to be famous to deserve respect.

Why should we not revere the boy who goes through school with an excellent record, who works hard at home and strives to achieve excellence in his examinations? Why should we not cheer on the girl who prefers to spend time each week helping out in an old people's home when she could be in a club or a bar with her friends? Why should we not hold up and admire someone who spends time raising money for charities rather than winkling cash out of their parents to spend on the latest designer jeans?

mature language used assuredly for the purpose

appropriate sarcastic reflection

fluency and appropriate use of semi-colon

effective short paragraph

repeated phrasing in the paragraph to challenge the audience

controlled and assured style and language

able to develop ideas with absolute confidence: links always effective and content handled assuredly

Examiner's comments

- This response matches form, content and style to purpose and audience. The writer seems perfectly in control of the ideas and can express them using different techniques and a mature vocabulary. Although this is only an extract, we can see the argument against making many famous individuals our role models; and the persuasion comes through rhetoric and the emotive mentions of individuals who commit themselves to worthy activities. Sentences, punctuation and spelling are worthy of the top band of marks.

Q5 We usually know most about those closest to us.
Write a **description** of a member of your family.

Extract from a C grade response

...However, when he was younger, he was very different. You can see it in old photographs and my father has told me a lot about him. He was wild and used to go round with gangs of 'rockers', as they were called. Sometimes he would get into fights. Once he even ended up in hospital.

He used to ride an old motorbike that was always breaking down and he would get home late and covered in oil. He never seemed to mind though, and perhaps that is why he eventually ended up opening the garage and working there all hours of the day and night.

He is happyest there. As he once said to me; 'Where else can you mess around with engines and get covered in mess and get paid for it? Its brilliant.' That is how he sees the job and because he enjoys it so much, lots of people take their cars to him to be fixed. He is a very popular mecanic.

At home, he spends a lot of time in the garden. That's not because he likes gardening, it's because my Auntie Sylvia makes him go out there, to get him out from under her feet. He spends a lot of time in his shed and we aren't sure what he does there really...

links to what has gone before

punctuation used accurately: here, inverted commas

sustains interest with detail

quotation to bring character to life/interest reader

sentences with different constructions

humour

purpose clear throughout: tight focus on uncle

Examiner's comments

- This response gives a clear picture of the man and it is in an appropriate style for the audience – in this case, the examiner. There are attempts to engage and sustain interest: the quotation and the touch of humour in the final paragraph of the extract. The paragraphs are linked well and the writing is mostly accurate.
- However, there are spelling mistakes ('happyest' 'mecanic' and 'its'), and the vocabulary is limited at times ('lots'). Richer vocabulary would have lifted the grade, as would more precise detail and development. For example, it would have been possible to develop the sentences 'Once he even ended up in hospital' and 'He is a very popular mechanic'.
- The response fulfils the requirements of the title without ever becoming exciting. There is a lack of originality (no similes, metaphors, irony and so on) and no real subtlety in the description – it would have been interesting to know, for instance, how the uncle feels about his banishment to the garden.

Q6 Write an article for a magazine that is sold abroad, **informing** the readers about how most Britons spend their leisure time, and **explaining** why.

Extract from an A* grade response

... The British, then, enjoy complaining, and wallow in the national characteristic of self-criticism. Perhaps it all has to do with their colonial past, and a feeling that they can never enjoy themselves: it is more important to suffer – and if nothing is currently imposing torment, they must torture themselves.

Ironically, they are also extremely patient in some ways, not least when they have the opportunity to queue. Whereas a Greek old lady will consider it a matter of pride to burrow to the front of any group waiting for anything and a Frenchman will shrug nonchalantly and wander off for a coffee until things subside, the Briton sighs with satisfaction and waits indefinitely for all those claiming priority to go before him. It has to do with school uniforms and standing for hymns and prayers in school assemblies for many centuries – the British constitution has been based on respect for order and understanding your place in the great scheme of things. So, the British wait. And wait. And if there is a line to queue in, so much the better.

Oh, the satisfaction to be gained from a good long queue! The sense of community with those around you, the excitement as the line edges forward! These are joys that foreigners will never understand ...

assured style and mature vocabulary

ironic style, continued throughout the extract

interesting sentence structures, perfectly controlled

light, mocking tone

assured control of style/content

sentence originality and variety

irony continues

Examiner's comments

- This is a mature response, where the writer displays skilful control in all aspects of his material: the form, with the development of ideas, all linked by the ironic tone; the content, appropriate and subtly presented; and the style, maintained throughout.
- The expression is always original, the sentences and the punctuation are varied and demonstrate a high level of technical expertise and there is a full range of appropriate sentence structures. For example, the waiting is emphasised by the sentences: 'So, the British wait. And wait.'

As with Section A of Paper 1, examiners concentrate on the **Skills Descriptors** when awarding marks. However, the other columns here give an indication of the sort of **content** they would be expecting to find when marking these questions. Compare your response(s) with the skills descriptors for each grade to find the best fit. Extracts from students' responses at grades C and A* are also included below to help you with this.

Grade	Skills Descriptors	Q1: *Two Scavengers* and one other poem	Q2: *from Search For My Tongue* and one other poem
U	• aware of the poems	• some understanding of content of at least one poem	
G	• simple comments • some detail • aware of some aspects of how poem is presented	• mention of people, their lives, problems or situations • simple response to presentation: e.g. 'There is a simile which says…'	
F	• simple comment, supported with evidence • relevant details • clear mention of presentational features	• accurate summary of one or two poems • begins to write about the people and the society: e.g. 'The scavengers are very different from the couple in the car…'	• accurate summary of one or two poems • begins to write about problems and situations: e.g. 'The woman feels she is losing her language and identity…'
E	• fuller comments • generalised comments on the texts • appropriate references/ quotations • comments on presentation	• begins to comment on aspects of language: e.g. 'grungy' makes them sound dirty…'	• begins to comment on aspects of language and structure: e.g. 'Gujerati is used so we know how she speaks…'
D	• some extended comments supported by references and cross-references • comments on effects achieved by presentation • aware of feelings, attitudes, ideas	• some focus on people and society in two poems and the language used: e.g. 'The stoplight immediately lets us know this is America and we learn about the society that…' • details used to support precise comments on people and society: e.g. 'The scavengers, compared to the couple in the car, are ugly: 'gargoyle Quasimodo'.	• some focus on identity, problems, situations in two poems and the language used: e.g. 'The problem is shown through the metaphors of death and growth…' • details used to support precise comments made: 'She is much happier at the end when the new tongue grows back.'
C	• textual detail used appropriately • clear cross-references • aware of poets' techniques and purposes • understands feelings, attitudes, ideas	• relevant comparison of how people and society presented: e.g. 'The different length lines show the fluctuations in this society, but in the other poem…'	• relevant comparison of how identities, problems, situations presented: e.g. 'The lines are not divided into stanzas, so we seem to just follow her thoughts, but there is much more organisation in the other poem, which shows…'

B	• textual detail used effectively • cross-references blended into the response • understands how a variety of techniques used • expands upon feelings, attitudes, ideas	• analyses methods of presenting people and society in two poems: e.g. 'The red light is "holding all four close together", and this allows them to be directly compared, but it is implied that under normal circumstances they would never meet…'	• analyses methods of presenting identities, problems and situations in two poems: e.g. 'The problems of dealing with a "foreign tongue", that is so different and makes the poet forget her own, are brought into focus for the readers when we are faced with Gujerati script…'
A	• argument has integrated references • analyses a variety of techniques • explores poets' ideas and attitudes	• analyses presentation, showing effects and effectiveness: e.g. 'The fact that they come from another world is emphasised when the couple in the car seems totally unreal to the scavengers – "some odourless TV ad"'.	• analyses presentation, showing effects and effectiveness: e.g. 'This other language, even translated, is alien to us, which makes us realise how difficult it must be for the poet to cope with two languages with no apparent similarities…'
A*	• response has clear message and development • detailed textual analysis • imaginative interpretation	• an original comparison, with the differences between the poems integrated: e.g. 'Whereas in Two Scavengers everything freezes into a picture, highlighting the contrast, in the other poem it is totally different…'	• an original comparison, with the differences between the poems integrated: e.g. 'Whereas from Search For My Tongue ends with an affirmation of the resilience of her mother tongue and her culture, in the other poem…'

Q1 Compare the way of life presented in *Two Scavengers in a Truck, Two Beautiful People in a Mercedes* with that presented in any other poem of your choice from 'Poems from Different Cultures and Traditions'.

Write about:
• what we learn of the people
• the kind of society in which they live
• how language is used by the poets.

Extract from a C grade response

…The society we see in 'Two Scavengers in a Truck' is one that is in parts. On one side there are the scavengers, but they are on a garbage truck and they are separated from and:

'looking down into

an elegant open Mercedes'.

The gulf between the likes of them and the rich is significant. Both sets of people are at the same stop light but have no real connection – the couple in the elegant car do not even seem to cast a glance at the poorer scavengers.

understands idea

textual detail used appropriately

understands message

We see a similar society in South Africa in 'Nothing's Changed'. There, the whites have a smart new restaurant: 'new, up-market, haute cuisine', while the poor blacks have to make do with a 'working man's café'.

In this case, we do not see the whites with the advantages, but we learn about the world in which they live, which has:

'ice white glass,
linen falls,
the single rose'.

This is made to appear fragile and beautiful, and is a total contrast to the world of the working blacks:

'wipe your fingers on your jeans,
spit a little on the floor:
it's in the bone.'

The poet appears to be speaking sarcastically, but the picture he paints is one of contrast. If people behave badly, it is because of the conditions. Probably the scavengers do not want to look 'grungy' either, but in both cases it is implied they have no real choice: this is their lot in life, whilst others have all the advantages...

cross-reference

appropriate detail

focused contrast: aware of technique

aware of attitude

clear cross-reference ideas clarified

Examiner's comments

- This extract reveals the skills required for a top C. There is appropriate textual detail, the poems are compared, the response shows understanding of what the poets are trying to reveal and there is some understanding of attitudes and ideas.
- To move to a higher grade, the candidate would have to delve more deeply into the contrasts – perhaps identifying the significant vocabulary in the contrast between the scene in the restaurant and in the café. He would also need to develop more fully the effect the descriptions have on the reader – and show, for example, how the gulf between the different ways of life in America are highlighted by the structure of the poem and the way the lines are set out. Similarly, rather than just saying 'the poet appears to be speaking sarcastically', this point would need to be properly explained.
- Throughout, this response is clear and detailed, but lacks the thorough analysis to lift it to a higher mark. It might have been more effective if it had been structured around the contrast between the apparently straightforward and objective description in 'Two Scavengers' and the subjective, angry narration in 'Nothing's Changed'.

Q2 In some of the poems from 'Poems from Different Cultures and Traditions', individuals are worried about their identities: who they are or who they seem to be.

Compare *from Search For My Tongue* with any other poem of your choice, explaining:
• the problems revealed in the poems
• how the poets feel about the situation
• how language and structure are used.

Extract from an A* grade response

> People living in alien societies have to come to terms with their surroundings and learn to cope in their new world. In 'from Search for My Tongue', Bhatt reveals one major problem, a metaphorical loss of her mother tongue, but indicates it is not insurmountable; whereas in 'Presents from My Aunts in Pakistan', Moniza Alvi appears to be lost in unending turmoil, as if she will never feel comfortable and settled.
>
> Bhatt's problem is, on the surface, one of language. Because she is using a foreign tongue, she feels as if her native one is dying in her mouth. Of course, this represents her whole culture, whilst the new culture is still strange to her. She feels as if she has:
>
>> 'lost the first one, the mother tongue,
>> and could not really know the other,
>> the foreign tongue.'
>
> A mother nurtures and protects us. It is a sense of safety that Bhatt fears she has lost.
>
> Alvi is in a different position. She does not feel as if she has lost her culture, because her past in Pakistan is still a reality for her, represented by the clothes, memories, articles around her like the camel-skin lamp, and her visions of Lahore. At the same time, though, she has adopted western traits, and longs for some western culture, represented through clothes again:
>
>> 'I longed
>> for denim and corduroy.'
>
> Such western styles are, no doubt, what her friends wear, and are very different from 'each satin-silken top' or the 'apple-green sari', the lovely but traditional clothes of her family, in which she feels uncomfortable:
>
>> 'I could never be as lovely
>>   as those clothes.'
>
> She is torn between worlds.

clear message around which the response will be built

clearly signals how response will develop

interpretation of problem

imaginative analysis

contrast

exploring poet's ideas

detailed textual analysis

She feels 'alien' because she does not fit in at all and seems trapped in her house, excluded as if 'behind fretwork at the Shalimar Gardens'; whilst Bhatt ultimately has a more positive experience, because she knows her original culture will always be a part of her, which is a relief. Right at the end, she says her native tongue:

'blossoms out of my mouth'

which suggests beauty and growth and a sweetness that will continue into her future...

clear development of ideas

contrast maintained

integrated references

interpretations

Examiner's comments

- The interpretations here are precise and imaginative, moving beyond clear comparisons into a more philosophical understanding of the poets' plights: how the language and the clothes represent a culture and how the poets respond to the complications resulting from their life in a different country.
- The response is detailed, with textual details integrated and used to illustrate and develop the points made.
- The candidate states his main point to begin, then goes on to clarify it. The message is clear and the development of ideas is logical. The response gives the impression that the candidate has a thorough understanding of both poems, can interpret and illustrate the meanings, analyse the techniques and handle two poems simultaneously and with ease.

These are exemplar answers which you can compare your own answers against. In English there is no such thing as one correct answer to a question; you need to decide if your answer contains the features needed to achieve a top grade.

UNIT 1: READING MEDIA AND NON-FICTION
1 Fact and opinion (page 5)

The first text relies heavily on opinion. It wants people to watch 'Behaving Badly 3', and implies that it is coming back with lots of confidence ('with a swagger'). It implies the stars will be doing fun things ('antics'), but that they will be 'despicable and downright dastardly'. The alliteration makes them seem amusing rather than evil. It describes the first show as 'a real stunner' to attract viewers, defines David Beckham as 'squeaky clean', sets up Colin Farrell as a 'bad boy' and says even Britney Spears is 'up to no good'. These opinions make the show seem exciting, since they might all be 'madder moments'. Such opinions, of course, are grounded in facts, such as what the show is about and who is appearing on it.

Whereas the first text relies so heavily on opinions, the second text begins with fact. As a newspaper report, it sets out exactly what is happening: who is collecting money, for which charity and why. Possibly to encourage people to help with donations, the report ends by printing the devastating facts related to the problems of Africa: 38 million hungry, 2.4 million dead in a year because of HIV, and so on.

The first text makes exaggerated claims, but the second text is more sober and serious. When opinions are used, they come from Graham, talking about the unfairness in the world and how charities can change 'this injustice'. He makes presumptions about other people ('the problems... are hard for us even to imagine'), and lays the blame on 'chronic poverty' and 'recurring drought'. It is interesting that he does not criticise governments and policies – but perhaps that would stop some people from donating.

In conclusion, the texts are very different, but suitable for their contexts. The Sky Magazine article is full of exaggerated opinions, to attract viewers; the newspaper is just reporting, factually, what Graham and Chris Lingard are doing and allowing Graham to voice his concerned opinion.

Comments An A* answer. Both texts are analysed in detail and their purposes and methods are examined. Facts and opinions are not just located, they are placed in contexts and seen as part of what the writer hopes to achieve. Details are quoted to support ideas. The candidate has understood exactly what is 'going on' in each text; they are compared well and completely. Perceptive comments on language and devices (e.g. alliteration) are made, and there is an awareness of the tone of each.

2 Following an argument (page 9)

The writer fears he is becoming old. He no longer enjoys Top of the Pops, and realises he is heading towards the final stage in his life. While he rails against the way Top of the Pops has changed and how the young behave, there is an understanding that this is bound to happen. In contrast, his son is there to show how young people think and act.

The text is structured around a conversation between the two of them. Much of the text is about how the TV programme has changed, but, rather than just explaining how age changes us as well, the writer demonstrates it. He is 'aghast' at the television, while his son just shrugs: 'So?' The 'half-naked girl' affects the writer's blood pressure, yet at the same time he feels like his grandmother, 'looking forward to going to bed'; but the son never bats an eyelid.

There is humour ('No drier in the toilet?'), but overall the text has a serious message. We are led to the rhetorical question we all have to face: 'What comes after that?' The writer uses the metaphor of the mint to argue that life is sucked away.

Comments An A grade response. The candidate understands how the writer is using the incident to generalise about growing old, losing touch with the young and their culture and yet fearing what that suggests. There is an awareness of the structure, though there could have been more analysis of exactly how the piece begins and ends. Quotations are used effectively and are integrated into the text, showing their importance has been understood.

In an A* answer, the informal style might have been quoted and examined: for example, how the writer uses sentences without verbs, for immediate effect ('Shock and dismay'). There is exaggeration too ('with rings all over') and details such as 'the Eurovision Song Contest' to make the reader smile.

The idea of finality is dealt with, but the harrowing image of 'madness and darkness' could have been explained; the mention of the metaphor is valid, but dropped in only briefly at the end, rather than being analysed.

3 Language (page 14)

The text is trying to attract people to visit Capri. It must be expecting the audience to be quite intelligent, because the first sentence is very long and the names could be quite confusing ('Sorrento, Positano, Salerno and Amalfi'). However, the paragraphs are just one or two sentences long, so they are trying to be more readable.

The writer uses some linguistic devices to make it all seem exciting. There is a simile ('mythological statues sit like sentinels') and Capri is made to seem special with the metaphor 'Capri is blessed'. It is also called a 'corner of paradise', so that sounds wonderful.

The writer makes Capri special but easy to get to. It is 'just' 20 minutes from Sorrento, and then there is just a 'short ride' by railway to the narrow alleyways of Capri town.

The advertisement is successful, because the language goes well with the pictures and it all seems summery and special, because it is like the 'Garden of Eden'.

Comments This is a C grade answer. Each bullet point is covered, and there is clear explanation of purpose and audience, some language features and why the advertisement is successful.

To receive a higher grade, the candidate would have had to be more precise about the intended audience (i.e. are all intelligent people being targeted, or just those with particular interests?) and to have analysed the language, explaining the religious effect of 'blessed', writing about what the 'Garden of Eden' actually suggests, linking it to the mention of 'paradise', 'precious' and so on. There could also have been emphasis on the history and mythology mentioned in the text, and the 'unspoilt' effect of the 'narrow alleyways' and the sense of isolation ('sitting off the coast').

The section on success would have been better if it had been related to purpose and audience, and had explained exactly how the writer was trying to persuade the reader, for example using geographical detail, exaggeration ('all eyes turn') and emotive description.

4 Layout and presentational devices (page 19)

The advertisement is trying to make the product attractive to men. Since many men would think skin products are made for women, the advertiser has attempted to create an advertisement that avoids features which are stereotypically feminine.

To begin with, most of the advertisement is blue, and blue is 'for a boy'. Also, it is not just any shade of blue – it is dark and a far remove from 'girly' pink. Perhaps it is meant to suggest the colour of a deep sea: that would fit with the idea of cleansing.

The various products related to Nivea face care are in the foreground and clear, so they might be recognised in a store, and they look straightforward and functional, not at all flashy. In fact, one is still in the box. Again, this might be to appeal to an average man who might be reluctant to buy a beauty product.

The writing looks similarly solid and 'basic'. The text is simple white against the blue; and the block capitals suggest stability, firmness and a lack of feminine curves. This even applies to the Beirsdorf logo at the bottom.

Each feature of the advertisement, therefore, is designed for men and it is hard to imagine it having any sort of profound effect on women.

Comments This answer begins by dealing directly with the question, and gives an overview of how the advertisement is intended to work. The conclusion sums up the candidate's opinion. Throughout, the comments are perceptive, and analyse, rather than just saying features are there 'to attract attention'. There is clear understanding of media techniques. The answer merits an A grade.

However, there is more the candidate might have added. For example, the positioning of the products is interesting – they are at the side, as if they are not being forced upon the target audience; they seem to have been placed casually there for anyone who is interested. At the same time, they look a little like a gang of friends, which might appeal to some. And, if the couple at the end of the line seem a touch apprehensive, hiding, that might be just like some of the potential purchasers.

The advertisement also breaks into two solid-looking, arguably masculine, blocks. Presumably, the idea is that the reader will read the text on the left, then glance down to the product and slogan below, which relate directly to the unexpected 'MOISTURISE' at the top. At the bottom, the details which are larger and stand out are 'NON-GIRLY' and 'ROUTINE' rather than 'face care' and 'sensitive skin'. It is assumed this will dispel doubts and win over male readers.

5 Selecting and using textual references (page 21)

First, the writer attracts women to the product by showing them looking happy. Then, she appeals to what women enjoy: 'gossip', 'scrummy comfort food' and 'a girls' night in'. Women are invited to make the most of the product by taking the phone off the hook and putting on the kettle: what many would like to do.

Along with this, the feature is trying to create an image of MüllerPud as the answer to the girls' dreams. By placing 'Mmm…' as a paragraph on its own, it seems to have been spoken by one of them. It sounds as if they are loving the taste, and is a sensual response that links well with the language used elsewhere, like 'delicious' and 'fun'.

This is a long way away from:
  'slaving over a hot stove and missing out on all
  the fun.'

There is also the use of alliteration and positive adjectives to make it all seem excellent:
  'scrummy crumble or succulent sponge, all served
  with creamy custard'.

This is just what many women would like.

Comments This response refers to appropriate details, such as the picture, and uses brief but effective quotations embedded in the answer ('By placing "Mmmm…" in a paragraph of its own…'). Longer extracts are indented for clarity, and the candidate demonstrates clearly how textual references should be used. The answer would be awarded a B grade.

Closer analysis would have lifted the grade. For example, there could have been comment on what sort of man is in the picture and how the women are responding to him – the inclusion of some sex appeal for the product. We also notice the MüllerPuds because they are placed centrally. Importantly, the heading is in red, linking with the 'müller love' heart, and the 'müller' in 'müllerpuds' below. Red might be seen as an indication of danger or something illicit, so could be tempting women to try the product.

The point about how 'Mmm' works is detailed, but there is little other explanation, and some comments are relatively limited; for example, 'This is just what many women would like'. Instead, in this case the candidate could have linked the description to the whole idea of a night in, spoiling yourself and indulging in luxuries that might normally be avoided – especially by women on diets. The quotation also has an adjective before each noun, and repeated 's's, making the whole experience seem slow and decadent, which might be very attractive to a hard-pressed housewife.

6 Analysing text types (page 25)

The advertisement aims to attract visitors to shop in Vienna, and is aimed at women. We know this because the shoe belongs to a woman, and the shopper is also a woman. She looks happy, which is meant to persuade us that we will enjoy shopping there too. The colours used are mostly shades of red, which makes the shopping seem lively and exciting.

The heading makes it seem that we can all get 10,000 Euros to spend. It then uses words like 'unique' to make Vienna seem special. We are told that Vienna has everything, 'From hip shopping mile to nostalgic old-city shop' so that everyone will be suited to it. Not only that, it seems vast with '20,000' stores. It is made to appear like the sort of place any woman would enjoy.

Lower down, it says 'BOOK NOW' and then makes the place seem foreign and exciting when the phrase 'Vienna Joie de Vivre' is used. In the bottom right hand corner, it looks as if Vienna is written in different languages. Then when it says 'waits for you' that seems handwritten, and is a friendly touch.

Comments The candidate deals with audience and the effects achieved by the layout and language and there is a clear attempt to engage with the media concepts. Purpose is handled too, though there is no mention of the campaign to attract shoppers in January and February, or of the 'prize' on offer. Significantly too, the 'shop & win' card is not even mentioned: and it is central to the purpose of the advertisement.

The candidate explains how some effects are achieved, such as when discussing the effect of the red in the advertisement or the 'friendly touch'. Other details, however, such as 'BOOK NOW' are described rather than analysed: there should have been a comment on the use of capitals, and on the use of the exclamation mark, to suggest urgency.

The response merits a B grade, but to move higher would have to be more precise in its explanations. It would have been helpful to examine what sort of woman is in the picture, and how the reader might suppose herself to be like this person if she were to shop in Vienna. The stylish shoe itself might be implying something about the quality of what can be bought in Vienna and the sort of people who shop there. Other points were overlooked entirely, such as the expression 'shopping spree', which again makes the experience sound wonderful.

7 Comparing texts (page 29)

Both sets of parents are under pressure from their children. They seem, however, to be reacting in very different ways, perhaps because their situations are very different.

Cosby seems to find it all a joke, and takes the opportunity to make fun of his wife and what she says. She thinks their son has done something bad:

"'I want you to be hard on him'"

but we get the feeling that she is not always so tough, and in the past has not wanted him punished:

"'Oh, please don't. He's such a little boy.'"

Cosby obviously wanted the child to suffer in the past, but now seems much more relaxed about it – perhaps because the son has upset his mother, not his father this time!

The lady who has written the letter, though, is in a much worse state. She is a single parent who has to handle it all on her own and says:

"'I am desperate'" and "'What can I do?'"

She is being driven to suicide by her girls and fears she might be sent to prison. She tells us about how her daughters treat her and how she feels about being used and shown up by them and having her money stolen. She does not appear to have done anything wrong and we feel sorry for her, whereas we are just amused by Cosby and his wife.

The lady who wrote the letter uses language like 'servant' and 'hotel' to demonstrate how she is treated. She also uses a lot of clichés like 'at my wits' end' and 'treats me like dirt'. This shows she is desperate.

In contrast, Cosby uses conversation to lighten the tone. He also uses funny metaphors, playing with the idea of 'washing your hands' of something ('Where is the sink..?'), then saying 'burn him now'. All the time, the child and what he has done seems unimportant. Cosby is having more fun laughing at his wife.

The humour even lasts till the end, when he jokes about children as being 'dark threats' (which they really are to the woman who wrote the letter), and criticises parents for being 'reckless' to create something 'as dangerous as children'. We do not feel he means it. But the woman who wrote the letter is not laughing.

Comments This is an uneven response, because the candidate has done well to contrast the different attitudes of the parents and to make regular comparisons, but has not analysed the language in any depth. Because of the cross-references, the detail and clear understanding of the parents' motivations, however, the response merits a top B grade.

To reach a higher level, the candidate would have had to explain, for example, how the metaphor of being a servant and the simile of the hotel were appropriate to the woman's situation; and why the clichés suggest she is desperate (perhaps because, under stress, she cannot think imaginatively).

More could also have been made of the metaphor of 'washing your hands' of a child – perhaps Cosby's wife is being compared to Pontius Pilate, who washed his hands of Jesus – and the way Cosby comments that his wife still 'sounded unwashed', as if her voice is her major feature. The ridiculous but vivid metaphor of burning also needed more explanation. The sense of threat at the end is dealt with, but should have been analysed more closely.

Cosby's use of conversation to bring the scene to life is only mentioned briefly; and other linguistic elements were missed altogether. The response could have shown how Cosby makes light of his wife's anger by using the metaphor 'she was singing this song now' and could have discussed his final, apparently contradictory statement ('as dangerous as children'). There is also the letter writer's use of short sentences, which show her desperation, and the final plea for some assistance which are not covered in the candidate's response.

UNIT 2: POETRY FROM DIFFERENT CULTURES AND TRADITIONS

1 Cultures and traditions (page 34)

There are no 'correct' pairings: any pairings are acceptable, as long as you have a clear idea as to how both poems focus on the given themes. In these answers, poems are compared with others from the same cluster, but you may use poems from either cluster in your exam answer. Also, you will probably be able to think of other themes apart from those suggested here. This list is just a starting point for your revision.

Cluster 1
Suffering:
Limbo – slavery; *What Were They Like?* – contrast between peaceful life and war
Others possible: *Night of the Scorpion, Blessing, Nothing's Changed*

Poverty:
Night of the Scorpion – family living conditions; *Blessing* – lack of water
Others possible: *Nothing's Changed, Two Scavengers in a Truck*

Inequality:
Nothing's Changed – contrasts between whites and blacks; *Two Scavengers in a Truck* – totally different lifestyles
Other possible: *Limbo*

Man and Nature:
Vultures – linked through love and evil; *What Were They Like?* – what the war did to the country
Others possible: *Blessing, Night of the Scorpion, Island Man*

Contrasting cultures:
Island Man – differences between past and present; *Two Scavengers in a Truck* – the rich and poor
Others possible: *Nothing's Changed*, any contrast between the cultures presented in the poems

Cluster 2
Living between cultures:
Presents from my Aunts in Pakistan – a girl struggling to fit into either world; *Hurricane Hits England* – realisation that the world is a whole
Others possible: *from Search For My Tongue, Half-Caste*

Language problems:
from Search For My Tongue – dealing with a new language; *from Unrelated Incidents* – linguistic prejudice
Other possible: *Half-Caste*

Changes:
Love After Love – how we alter; *Hurricane Hits England* – how our outlook can be changed
Others possible: *This Room, from Search For My Tongue, Presents from my Aunts in Pakistan*

Dealing with the unacceptable:
Not My Business - one person's attitude to repression; *Half-Caste* – how the poet sees prejudice
Other possible: *from Unrelated Incidents*

A positive outlook:
This Room – a cheerful vision of improvement; *from Search For My Tongue* – how language survives
Others possible: *Love After Love, Hurricane Hits England*

2 Content, attitude and message (page 40)

The poem is set in a hot country, where the people are poor and there is little water. When the pipe bursts and water shoots out, they become excited and rush out to collect it in anything they can. The children, meanwhile, play in it, delighted at the unexpected shower.

The poet has sympathy with these people, understanding their plight and stating simply:
   'There never is enough water.'

He describes the effects, as skin 'cracks like a pod', and shows how they dream of water, so that we can almost hear it:
   'Imagine the drip of it'.

He understands how important it is to them, because he describes it in religious terms ('kindly god', 'blessing'), while the people are like a 'congregation', in a way worshipping the water and what it represents in such a land. In fact, the water is seen as 'fortune', 'silver' and 'liquid sun', it is so valuable.

The message of the poem is that 'sometimes' things can be better. Of course, the way the people fight for the water shows how desperate they are; and though the children are happy when the water 'sings' over them, we finish with an image of their 'small bones' and know that soon there will be no water again.

Yet this is still much more positive than the message in *Not my Business*, where the suffering has no break.

Blessing presents a vision which has joy, if not long-term hope; *Not my Business*, in contrast, reveals violence in a society where the enemy is human but is faceless and grim. And whereas Dharkar sees the problem as one of climate and a lack of water, Osundare focuses on the evil of mankind.

> Comments This is an A grade answer which responds well to each section of the question. There is mention of the poet's sympathy, justification of how the water is shown to be important, textual references to show how the people react to the unexpected water and a conclusion which moves beyond simple detail, to explain what the poet is suggesting and how the message compares with that in *Not my Business*.
>
> To move to A⋆, the response would need more analysis in places, such as what 'cracks like a pod' suggests. Because the water is so valuable, it would have been appropriate to explain that it can be seen as the equivalent to wealth in other cultures and, arguably, is more important. Most importantly, although the final paragraph succinctly summarises how the messages of the two poems are different, there should have been a closer examination of *Not my Business* in order to produce a more balanced answer to the third bullet point.

3 Structure (page 44)

The poem is set out in two sections: the first asks a series of numbered questions about the people of Viet Nam; the second has numbered responses. The questions can be read together, as rhetorical queries; the responses also offer consecutive ideas. The questions offer a vision of the Vietnamese as artistic people:

> 'Did they use bone and ivory,
>   jade and silver, for ornament?'

Also, they seemed happy (with 'quiet laughter'), soft and musical:

> 'Did they distinguish between speech and singing?'

The responses present unpleasant answers, as 'light hearts turned to stone'. Each numbered response shows how their life and culture were destroyed:

> 'Sir, laughter is bitter to the burned mouth.'

The poem moves towards apparent death, as their traditions and happiness have all gone:

> 'It is silent now.'

The poem is structured in this way to make the reader remember all the qualities of life in Viet Nam before the war, then to reflect on the effect of the war on the country. The questions and responses are aimed to challenge readers and give them pause for thought: if this is the result, can such wars be justified?

The structure is effective, because the questions reveal a beautiful world, which is culturally distinctive and in which the Vietnamese are happy, at one with their environment:

> 'Did they hold ceremonies
>   to reverence the opening of buds?'

Then, the second section shatters the vision and violent language is introduced to shatter the peace: 'killed', 'burned', 'charred', 'smashed', 'scream'. In the silence, we are told there is just an echo of what went before – it seems to have faded as the poem has developed.

The poem can be contrasted with another poem dealing with loss: *from Search For My Tongue* by Sujata Bhatt. That poem also begins with questions:

> 'You ask me what I mean
>   by saying I have lost my tongue.
>   I ask you...'

In this case, though, the culture has not been lost. It is evident in the verse itself:

મને હતું કે આખ્ખી જીભ આખ્ખી ભાષા,

This device successfully shows the language as a living force; and this is supported through the poem by the use of the extended metaphor of a plant growing in Bhatt's mouth, around which the poem is built.

Unlike in *What Were They Like?* there are no sections. The verse has no breaks, to emphasise the continuity of the languages as the processes have no stopping. Also, the conclusion is different. Levertov's poem moves to a depressing finish, where all appears lost, but *from Search For My Tongue* ends with a confirmation of life and cultural identity, as the mother tongue 'blossoms' out of her mouth. It is a sign of hope and cause for celebration.

> Comments This is an A⋆ answer. There is consistent insight into how the poems are structured, noting the effects of the devices, and the candidate interprets significant details, such as the echo mentioned at the end of the poem. There is close textual analysis and carefully balanced contrast, saying how the poems differ, but also how they both achieve their success.

4 Language (page 50)

The extract from 'This Room' begins with bustling noise. There is an alliteration of 'p's and the onomatopoeia of 'pans bang', followed by an echoing rhyme: 'clang'. There is metaphor, too, because the items do not really 'fly by the ceiling fan'. However, the idea of wonderful change is reflected by these perceptions, and it is so dramatic there are even spectators, a metaphorical 'crowd of garlic, onions, spices.' This list and the sense of loud movements stretch through the first sentence, but it is all shown to be anything but frightening because of the brief but straightforward reflection to end the stanza:

'No one is looking for the door.'

Dharker feels as if everything is suddenly out of his control, and this is reflected in the enjambements that follow, which make his thoughts stretch out - yet, as we read the lines, the thoughts seem broken, as if he cannot concentrate. He is happy, though, as signified by the final line, ended with 'clapping'. The commas before the word makes the reader pause, giving the word extra emphasis.

'Presents from my Aunts in Pakistan' is much calmer. It begins with an internal rhyme ('saw Lahore'), which seems slow. It also seems to stretch out, perhaps like the girl's life. The description of her aunts' existence has none of the energy of 'This Room.' The poet uses the language of seclusion ('shaded' and 'screened') to describe how they are hidden quietly away. Instead of encountering the sharpness of 'garlic, onions, spices', which we can taste and smell and which affect the senses, in Alvi's poem the women are covering things and packing them away:

'wrapping them in tissue.'
This world seems safer, but lacks the 'excitement' that Dharker highlights.

Alvi actually ends with a vision of herself excluded from society, 'of no fixed nationality'. Her exclusion is symbolised by the fact she sees herself 'staring through fretwork', and she focuses on the lowest individuals: 'beggars, sweeper-girls'. By using such terms, it seems she associates herself with them.

The rhythm of 'Presents from my Aunts' is reflective and lacks the pace and energy of 'This Room'. Whereas Dharker is 'clapping', Alvi is 'staring'; as Dharker enjoys the 'excitement', Alvi stares through fretwork and is, undoubtedly, fretting.

Comments This is an impressive answer. From the start, poetic techniques are located and explained. Language, even some punctuation, is analysed for effect and is given a personal interpretation ('Instead of encountering the sharpness of...'). There is detailed comparison, dealing with a range of elements in both poems, and comparing them directly ('whereas...'; 'instead of...' and through the use of comparative phrases like 'much calmer'). The final paragraph cleverly pulls together key ideas and quotations.

Our understanding of each poem is improved because of the way the language has been examined. This response merits the award of A*.

5 Selecting and using textual references (page 57)

Both *Half-Caste* and *from Search For My Tongue* concern people who are uncomfortable in the society where they live. John Agard is angry, because he does not feel 'half' of anything, and sets out to prove he has as much right to be seen as a complete person as anyone else; Sujata Bhatt is worried because she thinks she is losing her mother tongue, through speaking English all day.

Agard demands an explanation for the way people speak to him: 'Explain yuself'. The problem is that if he is seen as 'half-caste' that is demeaning, and reducing his worth and standing. Because he does not want to be seen as 'half-caste', he produces a number of examples of how colours are mixed – in works by Picasso and Tchaikovsky and in the weather. Since none of these items are thought of as half-caste, why should it happen to him?

Bhatt's problem, though, is her own. She is uncomfortable handling two languages, which represent two cultures, and since she speaks in a foreign tongue she thinks her mother tongue could die, like a flower. She believes it dies and rots, and she spits it out and thinks she is left with only the new language.

Since she uses the metaphor of a flower to talk about her language, it shows she thinks it is delicate and beautiful. However, the metaphor is expanded and she reveals that in reality the tongue, like a plant, grows back in the night whilst she dreams. Indeed, it seems to be the superior language, because she says 'it ties the other tongue in knots'; and she sounds delighted at the end, when the mother tongue 'blossoms'. It is as if summer has come back into her life.

Agard, meanwhile, is sarcastic:

'Excuse me
 standing on one leg
 I'm half-caste'.

By making ridiculous statements, he is mocking those who label him. Bhatt's tongue comes back in a dream – but Agard says that he only dreams 'half-a-dream' and is not even a complete human being. Making fun of those who label him, he demands they come back as whole people to see him:

'wid de whole of yu ear
 and de whole of yu mind'.

It is as if they are the ones with limitations. Then, he says, they will learn he is a whole person:

'an I will tell yu
 de other half
 of my story'.

These final lines are in a stanza on their own, to highlight Agard's cynicism and anger. We are never allowed to forget the poem is about his bitterness about the idea of 'halfness', a concept that usefully frames the poem, as it is introduced in the first three lines. His use of colloquialism, lack of formal punctuation and use of speech patterns successfully help to identify him as of mixed race, but that never suggests he lacks intelligence: the references to Picasso and Tchaikovsky, and his use of words like 'consequently', in addition to the cleverness of his ideas, reveal the quality of his mind.

Bhatt's feelings are also shown successfully. Her mother tongue is used in the poem to show the reader what she dreams:

પરં તુ રાત્રે સ્વપ્નામાં મારી ભાષા પાછી આવે છે.

This shows us how problematic it must be to live with a difficult second language. What is clear, though, is how relieved Bhatt is when her tongue survives, and this is cleverly shown as it grows from a rotten leftover, to a stump, up to a bud, then a flower which blossoms. The poem begins with her unhappiness at having lost her tongue, but ends with its recovery and the relief of the poet.

Comments This is an A grade response, and both poems are analysed in some depth: it deals with people who are unhappy within their society; the poems are compared; and there is an evaluation of their success at the end. The candidate includes linguistic points and structural features, as well as providing a sympathetic understanding of the poets' feelings and situations.

To receive the highest grade, the response would have had to relate *from Search For My Tongue* more closely to the title's reference to 'mainstream society'. It might even have been easier to deal with that element if a different poem had been chosen (for example, *from Unrelated Incidents*, which is another protest poem dealing with prejudice in Britain).

Also, exactly how Agard uses Picasso, Tchaikovsky and the weather is never made clear. There is no reference to Agard's use of repetition – or to that used by Bhatt, who builds effects in several places by her repeated phrasing and the way she extends her sentences to provide a sense of wonder and excitement. Some points, too, lack clear analysis and explanation (eg. 'This shows us how difficult it must be...').

Finally, there needed to be a paragraph summarising the response.

UNIT 3: WRITING SKILLS

1 Generating ideas (page 62)

Your answer is likely to be based upon your own experiences. It is important, though, that you have developed the main ideas: at least three or four details should be included in each section. Having initially produced a quick spider diagram, your more detailed ideas might well be:

1. Teams:
Develop skills, fitness, teamwork
Football: all ages, each evening, matches at weekends, all welcome
Rugby: currently only for older students but could be extended, growth sport in the country, school matches all over the county
Hockey and netball: teachers enthusiastic, school has won lots of matches

2. Clubs and societies:
Convenient: most held during lunch break and lunch time, really popular (e.g. ICT and dance – modern, not 'Men in Tights'); plays performed recently

3. Trips:
Just this year: History to the Somme, Geography Field Trip, England international, French exchange, visit to German market, Spanish holiday – chances to escape lessons without digging a tunnel

4. Final positives:
Results in a Record of Achievement – useful when applying for jobs, and a way to unwind.

I wonder how long the British people are going to accept the waste of public money by central government. It seems incredible that so many millions of pounds are frittered away each year, whether we have a New Labour or Conservative Prime Minister. Surely, something could be done to use the money more wisely?

Just think about how much we spend on foreign wars and armaments. We keep rushing off to fight in distant lands, and it does not seem to matter how much it will all cost. Funding can always be found. *Yet*, that cash could be spent in important and more constructive ways, either at home or abroad. Do the politicians ever consider alternative spending plans?

Similarly, there seem to be hundreds of committees and enquiries that have lives of their own, and budgets to match. It is, clearly, a way for many individuals to make a good living – especially the judges and barristers – but what do these eminent bodies achieve? Should we really be prepared to sit back and allow our tax revenues to be frittered away for ever?

There are alternative ways to use the money. First, millions more could be invested in our schools, colleges and universities. Instead of making students pay their tuition fees, we could avoid going to war for a year or two. That would probably provide enough cash to keep the students going for ten years or more. *Then*, we could disband some of our forces and stop investing in more and more advanced armaments so that the hospitals and rail services could be moved into the twenty-first century. *What is more*, we would have extra funding for aid work abroad. It all seems quite simple if you think logically.

However, we need to act quickly. Every pound squandered is a pound that could have helped someone in need. It is time the people stood up for what is right and the politicians acted with more logic and humanity.

Yours faithfully…

main idea of letter and of the paragraph introduced at the start by topic sentence

topic of paragraph made clear discourse marker develops the line of thought and offers alternative

next topic sentence introduces a new line of argument

topic sentence is a general statement introducing the writer's more detailed ideas

discourse markers: 'First', 'Then' and 'What is more' structure the ideas and offer more alternatives

final topic sentence sounds the alarm and leads to the conclusion

GOOD POINTS:

- The paragraphs here have a logical development:
  1. There is waste and it should be stopped.
  2. The money could be better invested in other projects.
  3. Identifies a group of professionals getting rich off the waste.
  4. Alternative ways of spending.
  5. Conclusion: the need to act.

3 Sentences (page 71)

Q1 Clearly, there are a number of ways the sentences can be developed effectively. In terms of this exercise, the important point is that the simple sentences should not remain and that the text should continue to make grammatical sense. One possible answer is offered below:

'We knew nothing about the plans because the intelligence services, which are very secretive, told us nothing. It is all very sad because we could have issued warnings. We apologise and we wish we could turn back the clock, though that is simply not possible. We wish we could offer reasons, yet that is not possible either. We do know the people responsible will be found, and you can be sure that they will have to explain their actions so that then we might all feel better.'

Q2 There are any number of alternative answers to this question. Here are some possibilities. Remember, though, that examiners reward you for showing you can use a variety of skills. It would be unwise to both begin and end with the same technique.

1. opening or ending with a rhetorical question
eg. opening: 'Surely, we care enough to help, don't we?'
   ending: 'Doesn't it make sense to give charity a chance?'

2. opening or ending with a simple sentence:
eg opening: 'It is time to act.'
   ending: 'The solution is so simple.'

3. opening or ending with an exclamation:
eg. opening: 'The situation is desperate!'
   ending: 'We must believe the world can become a better place, and open our hearts and our wallets!'

4 Punctuation (page 76)

The problem for most single parents (men and women) [1] is that they have so little time to do anything but care for their children and work. Days are all the same: [2] make what seem like endless meals; [3] clean and tidy the house; work in an attempt to pay for next week's [4] food; and get as much sleep as possible. It's [5] a limited existence! [6]

But what can be done? [7] There must be ways that these people can make their lives a little easier.

'As far as I am concerned,' [8] said Mr Grayson, [9] who works for a government agency, ' [8] all we can do is make clear the benefits they can claim and offer, [10] wherever possible, support workers to help them through. Then it depends how the individual reacts...' [11]

Locally, [12] a considerable amount of money has been put into the system to help single parents – [13] over £500,000 - but it does not seem to have done the trick. Every single parent I spoke to was struggling. Perhaps Mr Grayson needs to come up with some more ideas? [14]

Comments There are rules to be followed when punctuating, but writers have some flexibility about exactly how texts are punctuated. Often slightly different punctuation produces a different emphasis. The answer above, therefore, shows some possibilities.

1. The brackets here are used to add information about 'single parents'. They could be replaced by commas or by dashes.

2. The colon is being used to introduce a list.

3. Semi-colons are used to separate the parts of the complicated list.

4. An apostrophe is needed because the phrase means 'the food of next week'.

5. Another apostrophe is needed here, but in this case it is an apostrophe of omission ('It is...').

6. The exclamation mark is used here to give emphasis. It would, however, be perfectly acceptable to retain the full stop, which would make the statement more matter of fact; or an ellipsis could be employed to make the statement fade away, almost like the existence itself seems to make people fade away.

7. A question mark is essential to complete the rhetorical question.

8. The speech marks go around the words actually spoken. The first part of what Mr Grayson says concludes with the comma; then, when he continues the same sentence, we use a comma, speech marks and a lower case letter.

9. Commas go around the additional information about Mr Grayson. Brackets could also have been used, but that would not have been ideal if they had already been used in the first sentence.

10. Commas go around the phrase 'wherever possible', which Mr Grayson uses to qualify what he says.

11. The ellipsis implies there is more to be said. It could be replaced with a full-stop or an

exclamation mark, if the writer wanted Mr Grayson to sound more 'up-beat', or to imply that seeing how people react can be quite exciting. Speech marks conclude what Mr Grayson said.

12. 'Locally' adds information to the main clause, which follows it. It is usual to use a comma to separate an adverb used in this way from the main sentence.

13. The dashes lend emphasis to the sum of money. Again, they could be replaced by commas or brackets here.

14. The rhetorical question ends the article. A full stop could have been used, but then the writer would have been making a statement, rather than questioning more directly Mr Grayson's range of ideas. An exclamation mark would have given the final sentence a more lively ending.

5 Vocabulary (page 79)

This is the candidate's actual response. Yours will, of course, be different.

My life in the hospital kitchen is very different from my existence at school. Within the prison walls of day to day life at my 'centre of excellence', no one bothers me. I can dream my hours away, gaze out of the window and imagine a knight in armour prancing over the fields to rescue me and take me off to some castle's splendour.

However, it is very different when I am working in the evenings at the hospital. As I slave in the pan room, over sinks of boiling water, there is no window. There are cooking pots to scrub and I am like an automaton: wash the pan, sterilise it, leave it to drain, move on to the next. Whereas in school a teacher might occasionally encourage me back to reality, in the steam of my nocturnal hell I am generally alone. There is just the intense heat, the sweat from my brow and the clashing of aluminium for hours on end. I feel like I am working in the bowels of existence.

Comments

- prison walls is not an original metaphor – a better alternative might have been endless monotony or unbroken tedium.
- a knight in armour... is full of appropriate and vivid imagery; and words like 'prancing' and 'splendour' suggest an extensive vocabulary range
- However could be replaced by other discourse markers, like 'Nevertheless' or 'On the other hand'

- an automaton: again, this is advanced vocabulary – your simile is likely to be different, but should probably suggest drudgery or boredom
- Whereas links the ideas; alternatives might be 'Although' or 'Even though'
- my nocturnal hell: this original metaphor would impress the examiner. An alternative of 'the kitchen' or 'the pan room' does not have the same effect.
- clashing or 'banging' or 'scrubbing' all use onomatopoeia to create the sounds
- in the bowels of existence is a particularly unpleasant image with which to end the extract. Your simile should also have been selected to have impact.

6 Spelling and accuracy (page 81)

Some of the words incorrectly spelt were included in the session, as important words to know. Others are regularly mis-spelt and deserve attention:

except – means to leave out. Correct word: accept
arguement – argument
exsessive – excessive
disapear – disappear
sychologicle – psychological
affect – effect. Affect is the verb, effect the noun.
doesnt – doesn't. Always remember to include necessary apostrophes (see Session 4).
ocasionaly – occasionally
choclate – chocolate
definately – definitely (stem word: finite)
vegatables – vegetables
losts – lots. Presumably a careless error.
improof – improve
ourselfs – ourselves
descent – means a route down. Correct word: decent
wast – waste
there – their
embarassed – embarrassed
too – to
childen – children. Another careless lapse.
sence – sense
hopeing – hoping
realy – really
truely – truly

UNIT 4: TYPES OF WRITING

1 Writing to argue (page 89)

Response 1

Bolton is not the worst place in the world, but it is not the best place either. It has a premiership football team and is close to motorways, so it is easy to travel around. However, if you are sixteen, you want more things to do and Bolton does not really have them. I like to dance and mix with my friends. I also love ice skating. It is not possible to do either of these activities easily, though, because we are not provided with meeting areas like handily placed youth centres or ice rinks. It is hardly surprising we do so badly in the Winter Olympics. Many people agree with me and feel that the local council should apply themselves to giving us more of what we want.

A good youth centre, for example, would get teenagers off the streets and into doing something more worthwhile. As well as letting us let off some steam in the evening, the centres could organise trips out to other places nearby, so we could try different sports, play against other towns and cities and so on. They might even take us to the coast in the summer or to the countryside in the winter.

Having these opportunities would change many youngsters' attitudes. It might mean they would feel more positive about where they live and they might be more willing to contribute to charities and things like that. Instead of mugging little old men and stealing cars, they could sit in comfortable surroundings and drink coffee and tell their friends what is wrong with their lives. Parents would be happier too, knowing that their sons and daughters are safe.

So, I would say to all you readers that it is worthwhile to ask for more entertainments and centres to be provided. If we all put the council under pressure, I think they will change their policies and make Bolton an even better place to live. I am already proud of my town. If we all work together, we can make it even better.

> **Comments** This response never really sounds as if it is from a real newspaper ('I would say to all you readers'), but has other features which mean it is worth a C grade. Even though the candidate deals with just one angle (young people's needs), there is some organisation: an introduction, paragraphs dealing with particular aspects (what is lacking, what youth centres could provide, the

effect they might have), and a conclusion which links with the opening. There is also an effective final sentence. Most paragraphs have a topic sentence; and discourse markers link some ideas (e.g. 'for example', 'Having these opportunities...' and 'So').

However, planning might well have been limited, because the candidate overlooks many possibilities offered by the title, such as how the town could be improved for a wider range of people; the paragraphs are generally of a uniform length, rather than being varied to support the subject matter; and at times some ideas do not seem to fit perfectly in a particular paragraph – for example, the sentence on parents at the end of the fourth paragraph seems a new idea which could be expanded and given a paragraph of its own.

The article might have benefited from the use of rhetorical questions; and there are no anecdotes or quotations. Although there are many details, there are no concrete examples, which would have added focus to the argument; but there is a touch of humour: 'Instead of mugging little old men...'

Response 2

Almost everyone who lives in Horbury will tell you it's a good place to live: 'It's grand here. Smashing little place.' It is quiet, green and safe; the little shops sell us everything we might need, the shopkeepers have smiles, a cheery word and time to look after us properly; and it is even perfectly situated for travel around the north of England, close to the motorways and a main-line railway station. In many ways, it is West Yorkshire at its best. Who, then, could ask for anything more?

In all honesty, many Horbury folk would like to see improvements. People are full of ideas about what could be done to make our haven much better, despite the generally positive feelings about the town. We pay our council taxes, so perhaps the council should listen to our concerns?

First, more senior residents need some sort of centre to visit and spend time with friends. The cafés are too expensive for them, and most do not want to spend all day in the pubs. My grandfather will sit in Boons' Pub nursing a pint for over an hour, but he would prefer to be elsewhere. All that he and his friends need is a warm building with tea-making facilities and a few comfortable chairs. They must have earned that in their lifetime.

Meanwhile, their children, the parents of the town, repeatedly complain about the state of the park. They want things for their children: a skate park without vandals; playing fields without dog excrement; a safe environment for even the youngest toddlers. The council should invest in a park warden and should ensure the police are visible to prevent any problems. A community constable on the beat would produce massive improvements.

Finally, there are the teenagers. What do they want? Only a theme park, multiplex cinema, Hollywood Bowl… Of course, they currently complain there is nothing for them but street corners, bus shelters and windswept fields – and they are correct. If they do not want to stay at home and lose themselves in video games, they have no alternative but to linger outdoors and annoy others by their very presence. The world has moved on and the young expect to have entertainment close at hand. A theme park is rather optimistic, but they would be more content if they even had a coffee bar or club to head for in the evenings.

We only live once and we all have a right to enjoy our time here. Horbury is excellent, but not perfect. 'Still, it wouldn't really take much to make it even better, would it?' said one old man. And he was right.

Comments This response, which is convincing as an article for a local newspaper, is worth an A* grade. It is well organised with a positive opening, logical development through planned paragraphs and an effective ending that summarises the content and links back to the positive view of the town and the improvements that are needed.

Topic sentences are used throughout; the discourse markers join ideas smoothly and appropriately; and paragraph length is varied. The rhetorical question that constitutes paragraph 2 changes the drift of the argument, moving on to a critical viewpoint; and the final paragraph is short to hammer home the message. Sentences and punctuation are appropriately varied.

Quotations are used in the first and last paragraphs, which contrast effectively; there are no anecdotes, but the image of grandfather in the pub is memorable; rhetorical questions are used sparingly; and there is a good use of humour, with the list of what the teenagers would like most.

2 Writing to persuade (page 94)

Response I

In Britain, we are living in a society that has a lot of money and where nobody needs to starve. People are paid well and most people have a job. Not everyone is living in a perfect state, but most of us have a roof over our head. It is easy to forget that not everyone is as lucky.

In the Third World, many people live very poor lives. They have to work all day for not much money and they cannot afford decent food or houses. Charities like Oxfam and Action Aid help them to help themselves, but we need to support the charities if they are to do that. An organisation like Water Aid only needs a small amount of money from each of us each month and they can provide wells and clean water. Can you think of a better cause? You should help them if you can.

What is more, even in England and Wales, some people still need support. There are some old people all on their own. The Salvation Army can help them. And there are drug addicts on the streets, with nowhere to turn. If we raise money for the charities that help them, we are doing our bit for our own society too.

It does not take much to be some kind of hero. My friend Katie did some fund-raising by doing a sponsored skip. We all thought she was crazy, but she managed to raise £85, which she gave to the St Mungo's Appeal, and will have made some poor people very happy over Christmas. You can even do a sponsored run, or hold a bring and buy sale. Every little helps.

It is better still if you get involved by helping to run the charity or actually care for others or deliver food parcels or even man the telephones. Doing work like that is better than sitting at home watching *Eastenders* or some reality show with second rate celebrities on it. If you help, you will be a real star, not just someone who wants to be more famous.

Comments This is a serious and sensible response, which has features that are appropriate for a radio talk. It is appropriately structured (our comfortable situation; then, problems abroad and at home, what we can do to help, and the personal rewards for helping); and it has a memorable ending. It might well persuade some listeners to help.

It also employs emotive language ('some old people all on their own' – which is one of several examples), rhetoric ('Can you think of a better cause?'), and an anecdote about Katie. There is an attempt to use repetition for effect at the start of the final paragraph.

However, the persuasive techniques could have been more in evidence. Although there is some variety in sentence construction, many sentences are relatively short; and the vocabulary lacks some variety ('people' is used repeatedly). The links between paragraphs are not always smooth and some ideas are not as precisely expressed as they might have been: for example, the final idea is appropriate but not expressed particularly effectively.

On balance, the response merits a top C grade.

Response 2

We take so much for granted in our lives. What we have, we hardly notice; what we lack, we desire. And yet we are the fortunate ones: we have a stable society, social care, heat and light, sanitation and houses, transport and employment, wages and pensions. If only everyone in the world could enjoy the standard of living that makes Britain such a comfortable place to live for almost all its citizens. And if only we in Britain would recognise our good fortune and begin to give more back to those in so much need.

What better way do we have to show our humanity than to become involved in charity work? It has its own rewards; we can reap our own benefits.

What is more, the organisations which look after the needy are crying out for volunteers and fund-raisers, and perhaps you could lend a hand. You could be the one the old lady smiles at when her meal arrives; or the one giving clothes to people who have a life on the streets and little more; or packing parcels to be distributed in any number of trouble spots around the world; or simply running a marathon to help research into cancer or Parkinson's disease.

Last Christmas, I took a step into the unknown and worked in a hostel for the homeless. It was grim, and the men who stayed there were broken. But they were grateful for a bed and some warmth and for just a few days they could escape the hell of their lives on the streets. I was part of making that happen – only a small part, but I would not have missed it for the world. And I know that other hostels need other

volunteers, and there is always a role for you, if you are prepared to give, rather than just receive.

The simple fact is that, whether you want to be directly involved or simply raise money, every charity will welcome your interest. But don't wait for tomorrow to contact someone; do it today. Later you might forget. Later, you might have changed your mind. 'Later' can sometimes mean 'never', which can mean a baby dies in Africa or a dog continues to be mistreated in Aldborough or a teenager cries in Altrincham.

Why not enrich your life by helping to make the world a better place and giving some of your energies to the world of charity? You can move clouds aside for others, see the sun shine down and feel its power in your own world too. It is an opportunity that is too good to miss!

Comments This response is genuinely persuasive and includes a range of techniques: repetition for effect ('If only...', 'Later...'); examples of what can be done to help; the anecdote about working in the hostel; rhetorical questions ('What better way..?') and a concluding exclamation; figurative language ('You can move clouds aside...'); and emotive touches ('the men who stayed there were broken').

It is well structured, beginning with a positive view of our own society and ending with a vision of how we can make dreams come true for others. It has a variety of sentences and the vocabulary is highly effective. It is of A★ quality.

3 Writing to advise (page 99)

Response 1

Dear Miss Knowles,

Now that we have got the extra money from the government, I am writing on behalf of Year 11 to tell you what we think you should do with it. £100,000 is a lot of money, and we think that if it is spent properly, there will be many benefits for the whole school.

We would like you to consider spending it in different areas – to improve the sports facilities, the computer room and the library. However, we also think the students would like some rest and recreation areas. We have some classrooms that are not often used. We would like to see those developed so we can use them as common rooms at break and lunchtime.

The sports hall needs new equipment, for gymnastics, volleyball and so on. If a chunk of the money is spent on improving it, the standard of fitness in the school might improve, which would be a good result. If more of the cash is spent on the dry play area and the fields, goalposts and cricket nets, then there is no doubt the school's sports results would improve too. That would help the school's reputation.

The computer room needs more printers and new mice, because students keep pinching the balls. Also, the library needs re-stocking and should have magazines each week, because that would encourage more students to go in there. Hey presto, our exam results would then start improving too.

Then, if we had common rooms as well, we would be out of the rain and better able to concentrate in lessons and we would not be hanging around outside in the cold. It would not cost much to provide drinks machines – which might even pay for themselves – and some games, like pool and darts boards. The students would then be much more positive about school and behaviour would improve.

So you see, if you spend the money in these ways, the school will be a much better place. We hope you take our ideas seriously.

Yours sincerely…

Comments The response is worthy of a C grade. It gives a considerable amount of advice and explains the results that would come from spending the money in these ways. Although they are rather brief and lacking in striking detail, there is also an introduction and conclusion; and the response develops through clearly defined sections.

The response generally is logical but does not necessarily win round the reader to accept the advice. It lacks the subtlety that might make the advice more appealing: positive examples of what has happened in schools with similar situations, for example, or even the implication that the school would not be 'changed', but magically transformed.

The paragraphs are somewhat mechanical and are sometimes not linked effectively (for example, the third and fourth paragraphs); and the vocabulary is sometimes not appropriate ('cash', 'chunk', 'pinching', 'Hey presto'). Many sentences are simple and the final paragraph is particularly disappointing – it seems as if the candidate just ran out of time.

Response 2
Dear Miss Knowles,
I am sure you will have no shortage of advice about what our £100,000 windfall should be spent on. On behalf of Year 11, however, I have been asked to summarise our views on this matter, and we hope they will be of some interest to you. We have been in the school for five years and are aware of exactly what it needs most; and, in addition, many of our students have attended other schools in the past, so they have experience of how particular facilities and improvements can be of enormous benefit.

It will come as no surprise that our priority is a Year 11 Common Room. That deserves financial support because it would remove some current and serious problems: foolish behaviour on the corridors by the troublemaking few; congestion in the yard; and students leaving the premises because there is nowhere for them to settle within the campus. To provide decorations, furniture and the conversion of the old gym, you will need to spend up to £20,000 on this development, but it will be money well spent.

Next, we strongly advise you to invest in sports equipment as this is in a chronic state. We can no longer play tennis using racquets with holes in them, or football without proper posts and nets. Our sporting results are already good, but improvements could make us the leading sports school in the area, and that would prove an uplift for the whole school – just remember the reaction in England after the Rugby World Cup. It is likely that the less academically inclined will respond really positively to these sports improvements. I am certain this advice will be supported by the PE and Special Needs Departments, as well as the main body of the school.

The remainder of the money can be put towards the new minibus – which should mean we will be able to buy it before the end of the year – and into computers for the library, which will help all those who go to the homework club each evening.

We feel that it is better to put significant sums of money into a relatively few projects, so that the impact is considerable, rather than spreading it thinly across a multitude of different good causes. We are confident that this makes good sense and hope that you will listen to our advice. Others will make suggestions to you, but we in Year 11 have experienced five years in this school; we know which problems are the most important to address.

Yours sincerely,

Comments This advice is offered sensitively. It sets out to win round the headteacher with logic (implying throughout that the students know what they are talking about); gives a full explanation for each suggestion; strikes a positive tone ('we... are aware of what it needs most', 'We feel...'); offers support (the PE Department and the Special Needs teachers); uses examples (the reaction when the World Cup was won) and effective details (racquets, goalposts and so on).

The introduction is impressive because it suggests that the advice will be based on sound knowledge, and the style is mature and convincing ('I have been asked to summarise...'). The different paragraphs develop logically ('Next...', 'The remainder...'); and the conclusion links to the introduction ('We in Year 11 have experienced...'), again emphasising that the advice is worthy of consideration. Throughout, there is mature control and variety in the sentences.

The response merits the award of A*.

4 Writing to inform (page 104)

Response 1

I love playing badminton. Once I have finished my homework each evening, I go straight down to my local sports hall. I am allowed to play badminton for as long as I want, provided no one else is waiting for a court. This is because I am a member of the Arnside Racquets Squash and Badminton Association.

I started to play when I was just six years old. My mum says I could always hit the shuttle but it did not usually go where I wanted it to. By the age of twelve, I was playing for the junior team and now I represent the seniors. I sometimes play singles when we have matches, and I am always in the doubles team.

We play matches all year round, because in our area there is no real 'season' for our sport. This means that once a month, on average, I play a home match and once a month I play away. That is always even more fun, because all the players in the team get on really well, and we have a laugh together. Once they even threw me in a swimming pool when we won our last match and avoided relegation. I think it was because I had done well, not because no one likes me.

I have won quite a lot of trophies. I was second in the county two years ago, in my age group, and have played in the national championships. Unfortunately I was knocked out early on. I had a cold and did not do well.

Anyway, in my bedroom there are twelve shields and some certificates framed on the wall. That is not to be big-headed, just because they inspire me to try even harder in the future.

Since I am so involved in badminton, I have little time to do anything else. My dad always says that isn't a problem, so long as I am enjoying what I do. My ambition is to play for England, and for Great Britain in the Olympics, and he approves of that, so I'll just keep on practising. I think that he is hoping I'll be able to get him lots of free tickets for the finals – but I just want to wear the team's track suit and win a gold medal.

Comments This response informs and is sensibly organised. Relevant facts are used throughout and, because of the nature of the task, there is personal response to accompany them. The information is suitably detailed and uses some more interesting touches, such as when the writer was thrown into the pool and his father's dreams of free tickets for the Olympics. The final idea provides a neat conclusion.

However, the language is fitting but 'everyday' rather than striking, the detail tends to be limited ('I had a cold and did not do well') and the response tends to be mechanical rather than exciting. It would have benefitted from the use of rhetoric, detailed anecdote or even quotation. Sentences could also have been more varied and complex. In many instances, such as in the first paragraph, sentences could have been joined and developed, to be more effective.

The response is worthy of a C grade.

Response 2

Both in school and outside, I spend most of my spare time on drama of one kind or another. These are not the everyday dramas of teenage relationships and forgetting homework – though I have some experience of those too – but the more serious kind: acting, performance, productions.

I attend a drama group twice weekly, audition locally and appear in at least two major productions each year. I have appeared on television too, which means I now have an agent and am hoping to get an Equity card in the near future: that will show I have been accepted as a professional actor and it guarantees me proper rates of pay!

My drama group does not put on productions. It exists to teach skills and allows us to improvise and empathise. The advanced class has been together now for almost four years. We know each other well and that means we trust each other, and can open up emotionally without fear or embarrassment. Jude, our teacher, says, 'It's all cathartic,' which means it helps us get frustrations out of our systems. I think she's right, and I always get back home feeling much happier about life.

While the group ticks on smoothly, the productions just keep coming along too. There are always advertisements for people to audition for serious plays and musicals, and I have landed some challenging parts. I've been in Osborne's 'Luther' and Friedrich Durrenmatt's 'The Physicists'; and I've 'Doh, a deer'-ed in 'The Sound of Music' as well as being a sailor in 'HMS Pinafore'. My friends sometimes laugh at me about my passion for drama, but, apart from the constant thrill I get from assuming a persona other than my own, acting allows me to meet so many girls that I think I am the one who should be laughing.

People at school certainly sat up and took note when I was on television last year. I auditioned for a part in a documentary, and made my television debut in a re-enactment scene. The programme was called 'Premature Burial' and was about what happens when someone is diagnosed 'dead' but is really still alive. I played a Russian boy whose uncle was run over by the secret police but survived. Mine was only a small part, but it helped me attract an agent, who has since got me various auditions for advertisements. Performing in these can be very lucrative so now I have another reason to develop my acting skills: my aim is to be famous and very rich by the age of 21!

While I am waiting for fame to call, I shall keep on doing what I have been doing because it seems to be my whole life. At times, I lose interest in other school work, but I have to persevere, because I shall almost certainly want to go to stage school or drama college, and the GCSEs will be essential.

Of course, if I am picked for the next Coca-cola advert, I shall have to think seriously about paying someone to do the exams for me…

Comments This response is very informative, well structured and interesting. It informs the reader about the writer's three areas of dramatic involvement, puts them into perspective by

showing that school is still important, and then moves to a humorous conclusion. The language is assured and mature ('cathartic', 'Equity card', 'lucrative', 'persona') and the range of sentence types is always securely controlled.

There is unusual but imaginative expression ('"Doh, a deer" -ed'), quotation, reference to plays and productions and a lively honesty throughout ('I meet so many girls'). Rather than producing a passionless response, this is information which draws the reader in with its enthusiasm and originality.

The response merits an A* grade.

5 Writing to explain (page 109)

Response 1
Everything that goes wrong for me seems to be connected to my friends. If there is a problem at school or at home, I have to sort it out by getting my friends sorted out first. That is just the way it goes.

Take getting to school on time. I always get up early, but then my mates come round to the house late, so we get to school late. I get into trouble from my parents if the school gives me detention, so I have to try to talk to my friends and make them understand what is happening. I even end up going to school on my own sometimes, when they look like letting me down. On occasions, I might have to grab a lift from Marcie who lives next door, and I don't like her parents at all. That's how serious it is.

My friends also used to get me into trouble when we were out at nights. Once or twice, the police were involved. It came about because we were hanging around the old people's bungalows, and they hated it because they thought we were going to break in and steal all their Abba CDs or throw bricks through their windows. Anyway, my parents made my life a misery again and grounded me for about a million years, so I told my friends we had to find a new place. Now, we usually have a laugh just down the road from the police station, which is quite ironic, really.

The worst problem I have ever had, though, was when I got a really nice girlfriend called Suki, and she said I had to choose between my mates and her. She didn't like them. She said they were a bad influence. One night she just said, "All right, what's it going to be?" I've never liked being told what to do, so I said I was just going to do what I felt like. That sorted out the problem straight away, because she left and I haven't been out with her again.

Overall, I believe I can deal with problems with my friends and can usually sort things out without making situations worse. Now, my friends are becoming more sensible all the time, so there are less likely to be problems in the future.

> **Comments** This response is of C grade standard. It is structured, the paragraphs are linked and it has a clear introduction and conclusion, which are linked through the reference to friends and the problems they cause. There is both cause and effect. Each situation is explained, we learn why it has come about and how the writer has reacted to it.
>
> However, the response uses mostly relatively casual expression ('mates', 'Take getting to school on time'), though 'ironic' is used correctly and there is humour concerning the Abba collections. In general, we feel as if the writer is talking to us in a friendly and fluent way, rather than demonstrating high quality skills. For example, note the repetition of 'sort out' at the beginning – it would have been better to find an alternative expression. Also, sentences are often simple and, although speech is included, the punctuation otherwise consists only of commas and full stops.

Response 2

Problems rarely have a simple solution, and that has been true of the main difficulties that I have had to face in my life. Looking back, I can identify two situations which caused me heartache and sleepless nights. Both of them were important because they concerned not only my own happiness, but also that of others.

Firstly, I had to cope with a grandmother who was living with us, and dying. She did not have any disease the doctors could cure; rather, she seemed to give up the will to live after a fall that rendered her unable to walk, and she just faded away, over the course of almost two years. She also developed cataracts that she refused to have treated and she eventually just about stopped eating. I had to be bright and cheerful around her and, increasingly, try to forget about her when I was studying or trying to sleep. It was the only way to survive, to support my parents and continue to care for my grandmother. I somehow managed to keep on top of my schoolwork and helped my parents by doing many of the things they no longer had time for, like gardening. This also kept me occupied, and my mind engaged.

It seems cruel, but when she died I could relax, because I knew I had survived. I loved my grandma, but, by the end, I was getting through the ordeal by treating her as a problem, rather than as a person.

The second major problem was when one of my friends, Alicia, died in a car crash and my best friend blamed herself for what had happened. She had allowed Alicia to go home with her boyfriend, even though he had been drinking, and he crashed his motorbike: neither of them survived. My friend had a terrible few weeks, crying and saying it was all her fault. All I could do was be there for her. I felt close to despair at times, but I listened, and tried to make her see Alicia had made her own decision – she should not blame herself.

Gradually, I persuaded her to go out again. I even arranged a date for her with my cousin and this was a starting point. She re-entered the real world. I did not feel proud but I felt relieved and glad that her improvement was partly down to something I had done.

I know that I have come through two testing times, but it is never possible to feel secure, is it? There will always be another problem, another decision to make, another person needing help. Then we have to start dealing with it all again.

> **Comments** This is an A* response, which handles two harrowing situations sensitively and confidently. We have the situations presented and explained, and there is a strong sense of the writer engaged with the incidents and engaging us, as readers ('it is never possible to feel secure, is it?'). The writing is detailed and the problems are developed so that we are aware of exactly how it felt to be involved and why she handled them as she did.
>
> The control of language is mature throughout: there is variety of punctuation, sentences and vocabulary. Ideas are linked and we progress from the introduction to the conclusion seamlessly, feeling that we have learnt a great deal from and about the candidate.

6 Writing to describe (page 115)

Response 1

Most of my life out of school is spent in the local park. That might not sound very interesting, but the park is where all my friends meet, and it has different parts, because it is so big. We can play around in the adventure playground, with its skateboard section; we can play football on any of the fields, or in the arena. We can have a laugh at people on the pitch-and-put course; or we can just frighten the ducks down by the lake.

Sometimes, when we are on the rides and swings, we must look like young children again, but we don't care. There's a slide that's about ten metres high, there's a roundabout that turns us into a blur, and a brilliant rocker that takes eight of us. We throw it forwards and back and you can hear the girls screaming at the other side of the park.

We go on the pitches too, but they are always full of mud which oozes over your trainers and makes the knees of your jeans stick to your legs. Of course, at weekends the nets are up and teams pour into the park to play league matches. There are blues and reds and whites everywhere, and people chanting.

At weekends, too, we hang around the pitch-and-put course, because it's even funnier than the bowling greens. Many of the old men playing bowls are actually quite good, even if they do all wear flat caps, but the pitch and putters mostly haven't any idea at all. On sunny days, there are kids running around pushing golf balls ahead of them (thirty hits to get to the green), women swinging and missing and men smashing the bushes about trying to find their missing ball. It's brilliant.

I know that the park seems like a strange place to spend all your time, but it's better than just watching television, and it's not all the same. In fact, when the fair comes in summer and it's full of frying onions and rides, it's one of the best places in the world.

> Comments This response describes the different parts of the park and what goes on there, and the candidate has included use of the senses: what you see, hear (screaming, chants,) touch (the oozing mud) and smell (onions). The candidate responds to the title by reflecting on why he enjoys this place.
>
> It is structured sensibly, moving from one area to the next, and has an introduction and conclusion.
>
> There is little imagery, though, with just the metaphor 'turns us into a blur'. The vocabulary is appropriate and suitable, but not particularly effective: 'brilliant rocker', 'It's brilliant'. The response would have benefitted from more variety in expression and from the inclusion of some

speech, similes or anecdotes. It fulfils a function, without ever being exciting or especially interesting. The mention of the fair at the end seems like an idea that has been added on, but it might have provided more interesting material for the writer if it had been extended.

> Overall, the response merits the award of grade C.

Response 2

Many places in which we spend a good deal of our time offer little of real interest: the local shops, the city centre, the bus shelter at the end of the road. We tend to think of our everyday environment with a shrug, and although we know these places have features, we often no longer register them, because we know them so well. However, when you also spend a good deal of your time somewhere very different, that place can seem to exist in more vibrant colours and offers more distinct impressions. This is the case for me with Croyde in North Devon.

My family and I do not only go to Croyde because it has such a beautiful beach, although that is one of its attractions. The sand stretches soft and long and yellow around the bay, and the sea lures surfers from all over the country. We love the crashing waves, the grasses rustling in the sand dunes and the water courses running down from the hills, across the beach and into the sea; but there is more to Croyde than the beach…

At the end of the road to the coast lies Ruda, a camping and caravan park like no other. It is spotlessly clean, and it includes a leisure complex that should be a template for other such sites around the country. There are numerous bars, entertainment daily for both children and adults, and restaurants bursting with exotic menus.

Beside it, the Ruda Pool is cheap to enter and exciting. The smell of chlorine hovers around the immediate area, but that is hardly surprising because it opens from the conventional tropical inside onto a sunshine area outside; and it has a slide, waves and two giant racoons parading around and enlivening the holiday for children. It is open until late in the evening, and screams are still coming from the building at nine o'clock at night.

Back up the road lies Croyde village: once sleepy, no doubt, but now pretty and old and offering good food and the finest ice-cream shop this side of the Atlantic.

Miraculously, the village rarely jams with traffic and rarely tastes of exhaust fumes. Instead, it is sunny and green and full of richness. The houses are of stone, animals are within metres of the village centre and, despite the visitors that flood the area in summer, it continues to embody a rural life that we usually have to read about in old books.

It is because of these things that we love Croyde and travel there so often. It is the sort of place that gets inside you and stays there; it spices your dreams when you are away and welcomes you when you return. The thought of going back can make even the local shops, the city centre and the bus shelter more bearable.

> **Comments** This is an effusive but maturely written description that is awarded A*. It has a philosophical but not irrelevant opening, to which the writer returns for the touch of humour at the end of the final paragraph. We are led through the different parts of Croyde that are described, and there is use of the senses, including effective onomatopoeia ('crashing', 'rustling'). There is metaphor too ('tropical', 'sleepy', 'spices your dreams') and alliteration ('stretching soft'). There is a range of discourse markers (including 'Miraculously') and the vocabulary is assured and confident ('luring', 'template', 'enlivening', 'embody').

6 Blending types of writing (page 119)

1. Some say it's not necessary/not possible: feel healthy anyway, convenience foods make life easier, no time for exercise, no need to worry when you're young
2. It is important to lead a healthy life when you're young as this affects your life when you are old; teenagers who sit around in front of the television and eat junk food are overweight and often suffer from emotional problems too. As schools do not provide much sport and often have chips and burgers for lunch, must be healthy at home in the evening and at weekends.
3. Benefits — immediate improvements we all notice: energy increased, more alert, happier. Examples of older people who look younger because they were healthy as teenagers.
4. Need to start immediately, rather than putting it off. Try to get a friend to make similar efforts. Start eating more fruit and vegetables, fit exercise into the daily routine, cut down on alcohol and smoking, avoid excess sun. Log all-round improvements in weight, exercise capability and emotional response, to encourage yourself to continue.

> **Comments** As with the examples within the session, this structure would need to be supported by an introduction and conclusion. It then starts with argument, by placing two distinct points of view. Persuasion begins to emerge at the beginning of section 2, but extends further in section 3, which presents ideas intended to appeal and convince. Finally, section 4 offers advice which links back to the problems identified in section 2.

INDEX

indentation
    in poetry 41
    for textual references 20
inferences in unseen texts 13
informality
    comparing texts 12
    in writing tasks 77
    see also colloquial language
information writing 100–4
    blended with other types 118,
        119
instructional writing, vocabulary in
    10
introductions
    in argumentative writing 6,
        85–6
    in writing tasks 63, 64
        advice writing 95, 98, 99
        argumentative writing 85–6
        descriptive writing 110, 111,
            114, 115
        explanation writing 105, 108,
            109
        information writing 100
        persuasive writing 90
inverted commas
    for textual references 20
    in unseen texts 11
    see also speech marks
irony 12, 13
    argumentative writing 9
Island Man 33, 53–4, 55, 56

language
    in poetry 45–50, 51–4
        and culture 32
    in unseen texts 10–14
        argumentative writing 7–9
        autobiographies 24–5
        comparing texts 27–8
        news reports 22
    in writing tasks
        advice writing 99
        descriptive writing 113
        explanation writing 106,
            107–8
        information writing 102, 103,
            104
        persuasive writing 91, 92, 94
    see also tone; vocabulary

layout 15–19
Leonard, Tom 32, 41
Levertov, Denise 32, 33, 44
Limbo 33, 43, 45–6
linguistic devices
    in unseen texts 11–12
    see also alliteration; metaphors;
        onomatopoeia; similes
linking paragraphs 65–6
lists
    in argumentative writing 88
    in poetry 48, 49, 51, 52
    punctuation for 74
    in unseen texts 13
logos 15, 23
Love After Love 34, 47–8

media
    reading 2–29
    technical terms 15–19
message in poetry 31, 35–40
    and language 47–8
metaphors
    in poetry 37, 46, 49, 53
    in unseen texts 11–12, 23
    in writing tasks 78
        descriptive writing 112
modal verbs 107–8

news reports 22–3
    technical terms 15–19
Nichols, Grace 33, 45, 53–4, 55,
    56
Night of the Scorpion 33, 42, 43,
    45
non-fiction, reading 2–29
Nothing's Changed 33, 43, 51–2,
    54, 55
Not My Business 32, 37–9, 43

onomatopoeia
    in poetry
        Island Man 53, 56
        Limbo 46
        Nothing's Changed 51, 52
        This Room 48, 49
    in unseen texts 11, 12
    in writing tasks 78
opinion 4–5
    comparing texts 27–8

in information writing 101, 103,
    104
organisation
    poetry 42–3
    writing tasks 82–3
        information writing 100
        paragraphs 65–6
    see also planning
Osundare, Niyi 37–9

paragraphs
    and speech marks 73
    in unseen texts 10
        news reports 22, 23
    in writing tasks 58, 63–7
        advice writing 95–6
        argumentative writing 86
        descriptive writing 110
        explanation writing 105, 107
        information writing 100
        persuasive writing 90
people in poetry 33
personal responses in information
    writing 102–3, 104
persuasive writing 90–4
    blended with other types 116–17
    rhetorical questions in 71, 92, 94
    unseen texts 10
pictures 15, 16, 18, 22
    web pages 23, 24
planning 60–1, 63
    advice writing 95–6
    argumentative writing 86
    descriptive writing 110
    explanation writing 105
    information writing 100
    persuasive writing 90
poetic techniques 45–6
poetry 30–57
points of view/viewpoint
    in argumentative writing 84–9
    in persuasive writing 90, 94
    in unseen texts 6
presentational devices 15–19
    and poetry 41
    and purpose 17–18
    see also structure
Presents from my Aunts in Pakistan
    32, 49, 50
problems in poetry 33